Praise for
When Your Parent Becomes Your Child

"Extraordinarily moving and triumphant—Ken has given us an inspiring and informative account, laced with humor and a thoughtful message about human dignity, belief in God, and love for the people who have sacrificed so much for us."

"With America's Baby Boomers just now hitting retirement age, more American families than ever are finding themselves stuck in the unexpected position of having to parent their parents. This creates a world of emotional and physical challenges that most people haven't considered, but are probably walking right into. In *When Your Parent Becomes Your Child*, Ken Abraham opens up about his own journey with his mother and helps us get a sense of what to expect. It's a must-read for anyone with parents over sixty."

> —DAVE RAMSEY, *New York Times* best-selling author and nationally syndicated radio host

"I love Ken's heart, as well as his writing, and I love how poignantly he addresses this delicate subject of caring for aging loved ones. As individuals live longer, families need long-term support navigating the joys and challenges that come with loving each other for the long haul. Keep this resource close. It is a treasure."

> —BILL GAITHER, ASCAP Gospel Songwriter of the Century

"I have counseled many families that have taken this emotional journey. Each one has a story to tell and Ken has captured their hopes and fears through his words. His honesty of denial through acceptance is courageous. It will certainly be an inspiration to others going through the progression of this disease that robs not just the person but those that love them of life's memories."

—STEPHEN J. D'AMICO,
MD, CMD

"Ken's thoughtful and transparent approach to this very difficult subject will give understanding and hope to many."

—DAN MILLER, best-
selling author of *48 Days
to the Work You Love*

"Abraham, a good storyteller, makes incidents of his family's journey come alive, and the book is immensely readable. . . . Abraham has chosen to engage readers with a vivid account that many can relate to. He offers an honest message of sympathy, solidarity, and faith that can be used in trying circumstances."

—*Publishers Weekly*

When Your
PARENT
Becomes Your
CHILD

A Journey of Faith *Through My Mother's Dementia*

KEN ABRAHAM

THOMAS NELSON
Since 1798

NASHVILLE DALLAS MEXICO CITY RIO DE JANEIRO

Published in Nashville, Tennessee, by Thomas Nelson. Thomas Nelson is a registered trademark of Thomas Nelson, Inc.

Published in association with the literary agency of Mark Sweeney & Associates, Bonita Springs, Florida 34135.

Thomas Nelson, Inc., titles may be purchased in bulk for educational, business, fundraising, or sales promotional use. For information, please e-mail SpecialMarkets@ThomasNelson.com.

Lyrics:

"What a Day That Will Be," Words and Music by Jim Hill © 1955, © renewed by Ben L. Speer. All right reserved and controlled by Ben Speer Music. Used by permission.

"Victory in Jesus," E.M. Bartlett © 1939 by E.M. Bartlett. © renewed 1966 by Mrs. E.M. Bartlett. Assigned to Albert E. Brumley & Sons/SESAC (admin. ClearBox Rights). All rights reserved. Used by permission.

"Sweet, Sweet Spirit," Doris Akers © 1962, Renewed 1990. Manna Music, Inc. ASCAP (admin. ClearBox Rights). All rights reserved. Used by permission.

Library of Congress Cataloging-in-Publication Data

Abraham, Ken.
  When your parent becomes your child / by Ken Abraham.
    p. cm.
  Includes bibliographical references.
  ISBN 978-0-8499-4727-8 (trade paper)
  1. Dementia—Patients—Care. 2. Alzheimer's disease. 3. Dementia—Patients—Family relationships. 4. Dementia—Religious aspects—Christianity. I. Title.
  RC521.A27 2012
  362.196'83—dc23   012020383

Printed in the United States of America

13 14 15 16 17 QG 6 5 4 3 2

CONTENTS

CONTENTS

Minnie . . . before dementia stole her freedom.

Chapter 1

THE MEN IN WHITE SUITS

How is it possible to lose a loved one while he or she is still living, still sitting right in front of you, talking with you, smiling at you—and yet the person you have known and loved for years is somehow gone? You observe the subtle quirks and idiosyncrasies that are occurring with ever-increasing frequency, yet you are oblivious to the truth—that you are not dealing with the obstinacies or unintentional offenses of an elderly person; you are facing a devastating disease and possess few tools with which to fight it.

Others noticed the changes in my mom before I did. Dave Saunders, a friend who attends the same church as our family, observed Mom shuffling across the atrium toward the main sanctuary. "Did something happen to your mom?"

"No, what do you mean?"

"She seems to be moving much more slowly than when she was here visiting the last time," Dave observed.

"Yeah, she's slowing down a step or two," I agreed. I hadn't really noticed the difference that much since it was such a gradual process, but others who had not been around Mom could tell that she had changed. That was my first clue that something wasn't right.

Mom's demeanor should have piqued my suspicions after the thirteenth phone call—all in the same morning—but I was oblivious to her true condition. She didn't really need anything; she just wanted to say hello, which she had done in calls number one, two, and three, none of which she remembered dialing. The remaining calls were more of the same, all recorded on my voice mail.

"Ken, this is Mom. Just wanted to let you know that I had a good breakfast. Bacon and eggs, toast, and prunes. Lots of prunes."

"Oh, that's great, Mom. I'm glad you are eating well."

The second call was identical to the first, and the eleventh, twelfth, and thirteenth calls brought little variation. My brothers had warned me, but I had steadfastly resisted the idea that my mother, now eighty-five years of age in 2007, was not as mentally alert as she had always been. Oh, sure, I had seen signs, but had chosen to interpret them as merely her quirky way of doing things. I hadn't lived near my mom for more than twenty years, so her idiosyncrasies and peccadilloes seemed more humorous than irritating to me.

I'd noticed some paranoia whenever she'd visit us from Orlando, but I always shrugged off her fretting as simply the fears—real and imagined—of an elderly person who was in a strange environment.

One night, around midnight, she called out for me. "Ken, there's a man standing down at the front of the driveway."

"Wah . . . huh?" I was half asleep. "No, Mom, there's nobody out there. Go back to bed."

"He's right there, Ken. I can see him, plain as day!"

I got out of bed and went to the window, not really expecting to see anything, but willing to check anyhow. I peered out the window into the darkness. Nothing. "There's nobody there, Mom. Go to sleep."

"I'm not going to sleep with some man down there staring in your windows!"

"Mom . . ."

I'm not sure which of us was more exasperated, Mom or me. She insisted somebody was snooping around our home, out at the front of our driveway. "He's right there!" she fretted.

"Mom, there's nobody out there," I said emphatically, putting my glasses on so I could see more clearly, just to make sure.

"Look, there he is," Mom said nervously. "He's moving; he's over there now, standing right at the front of the driveway!"

I pressed my face up closer to the window and rubbed my eyes as I stared into the darkness again. I didn't see a thing in the driveway, although I noticed the breeze blowing the treetops a bit, creating some unusual shadows on the ground. There was only one thing to do. I turned around and grabbed my mother's hand. "Come on, Mom. We're going down there."

Now don't get the impression that I'm some sort of Rambo character, ready at a moment's notice to go kick some butt. No, I don't usually go looking for trouble. But I wasn't worried; I could see clearly from my front windows that there was no trouble in the driveway. A streetlight was a mere ten feet away from the entrance to our driveway, illuminating the area sufficiently to show that nobody was out there. But Mom was convinced that a man was standing by our mailbox, so I was intent on proving to her that she was seeing things. "Come on," I said. "We're going down there."

"No!" she cried. "He might be dangerous. Maybe he has a gun or a club or something."

"Mom, nobody is there, and I'm going to show you that. Trust me. Come with me." I tugged her toward the front door.

Reluctantly, my mom followed me out the door and down the steps to the sidewalk leading to our driveway. She trudged as slowly as I would allow her, reluctantly traversing the entire length of the driveway, about one hundred feet. When we finally arrived at the front of our property, I put my arm around her shoulder, and stretched out my hand, pointing in every direction. "What do you see, Mom?"

"Nothing."

"What about over there?"

"No, there's nothing there."

"And what about that way?"

"Ken, I saw it. There was a man down here, and he was looking up at your house."

Just then the breeze blew through the trees, causing the leaves to cast an eerie shadow on the entrance to the driveway. Wanting to placate her, yet at the same time hoping to allay her fears, I said, "Maybe that's what you saw, Mom. The leaves rustling in the wind. See how the tree casts a shadow over the mailbox? I can understand how you might have thought that you saw somebody, but I want you to understand that there is nothing to fear."

She stared at the tree, and then at the shadows on the brick entryway. "Maybe that's what I saw," she conceded.

"Yep, probably so. Let's go back inside and get some sleep." I felt good. I had kindly yet firmly convinced her that her fears were groundless. My exaltation lasted only a few seconds. Walking back up the driveway, I heard her mumble, "He could be hiding down there in the bushes somewhere, or maybe he ran off into the woods."

It wasn't worth arguing about.

That was the first of many similar incidents. Most of them were innocuous, with Mom waking us up in the middle of the night, worried that there were men in white outfits outside in our yard. Once she got so upset she started crying. "I'm not lying, Ken. There are men out there, at least six or seven of them, and they are wearing white uniforms. I saw them!"

Seeing the hurt in her eyes nearly crushed me. "I believe you, Mom," I said, wrapping my arm around her shoulder. "I believe you saw something, but look; there's nothing there."

A few nights later I was working in my office when I heard her call out from the guest bedroom upstairs. "Ken! Come quickly. They're shining their lights on my window." I bounded out of my chair and ran up the stairs to where Mom was standing in the darkness, dressed in her nightgown, scared stiff. "There." She pointed to the window. "Do you believe me now? Look right there."

I looked at the closed venetian blinds covering the window, and clearly there was no light shining on them. "I don't see a thing, Mom."

"Right there!" she shrieked quietly. "Can't you see that light right there? It's moving up and down the blinds."

I looked again. At nothing.

"There isn't anything there, Mom. No light, nothing."

"Ken, just look." She sounded exasperated.

I went over to the blinds, opened and closed them, raised the blinds so I could look out the window. Nothing. "There's nothing there, Mom."

"But I saw it!"

"I believe you saw something, Mom. Maybe your eyes are acting up, or you're developing a cataract problem again, like you had when you were younger. But there's no light and there's nobody out in the yard. I can see because of the streetlight shining in the yard, and I'm telling you, there's nobody out there."

Mom went back to bed, and I went back to work, gloating in my small victory—I had convinced my mom that what she was seeing did not exist. I had no clue that it is almost impossible to convince a person with dementia that he or she is wrong; your only hope of diffusing the situation is to redirect the conversation. But at the time I had no idea that Mom had dementia.

We learned the hard way that it was no longer safe to leave Mom alone. One night during her visit, my wife, Lisa, and I were scheduled to attend a wedding and sit-down dinner reception. Although we often took Mom along to church events, weddings, graduations, baby showers, and other celebrations, this invitation did not include her, so we felt that it would be inappropriate to take her with us. We even considered not going ourselves because we didn't want to leave my mother alone.

"Oh, I'll be fine," she reassured us. "I'm not afraid to be alone for a while. Hey, I live by myself in Florida. You two go and have a good time."

"Well, okay," I said, with visions of men in white suits dancing through my mind. "We're going to the wedding, but we won't be long. We'll be back around eight o'clock. Call me on my cell phone if you have any problems or need anything."

The wedding ran a little longer than anticipated, and although we stayed only briefly at the reception, it turned out to be just long enough for our home to be surrounded by the men in white uniforms. Shortly after 8:00 p.m., Lisa and I left the reception and headed home. As I drove, we got caught up talking merrily about what a beautiful wedding and reception it had been, and I completely forgot about checking my cell phone messages. We were only fifteen minutes away from home, so I didn't even think about turning my phone back on. Until we pulled down the road leading to our driveway. The moment I saw the flashing red lights atop the police car in our driveway, my heart nearly stopped.

I pulled in behind the police car, jumped out of our vehicle, where I was met by two armed police officers. "Mr. Abraham?"

"Yes, sir."

"Mr. Abraham, I'm Officer Thomas, and this is Officer Jones. Your mother called us and reported that there were intruders around or inside your home. We responded immediately to the call, and we searched every room in your house. There are no intruders, and nothing seems to be disturbed."

Nothing except Mom, I thought. "Thank you, gentlemen. I really appreciate you watching out for us. My mom gets a little nervous these days."

"You're an author, huh?" Officer Thomas asked.

"Yes, sir, I am."

"Yeah, your mom showed us around your office. You have quite a library. And your name is on a lot of books."

"Er . . . ah, yes, my mom is rather proud of me."

"She sure is," Officer Jones chimed in. "She showed us every book you've ever written."

"She did?" At that time, I'd written more than seventy books.

"Oh, yeah, she sure did."

"Well . . . ah, thanks again, officers. I'm sorry she bothered you."

"Oh, no bother, Mr. Abraham. Nice to meet you." The policemen waved and walked to their car.

"Ah, yeah . . . nice to meet you too." I forced a smile as I waved good-bye to the officers and moved my car so they could get around me.

Once inside the house, I confronted my mom. "Mom! What in the world were you thinking? Why did you call the police?"

Mom was immediately defensive. "I didn't call the police. I called 9-1-1."

"Around here, that's calling the police!"

"Well, there were men outside in the yard, and I got scared."

"Mom!"

"And those policemen, the first thing they asked me when they came up on the porch and I answered the doorbell was, 'Ma'am, are you on any medication?' They didn't ask about the prowlers; they didn't ask me if I was hurt. All they asked was whether I was taking medication. What do they care whether or not I'm on medication? It's none of their business."

"Maybe not, Mom," I said. "But it is their business when people call them out on false alarms, when there's no real threat of danger."

"I didn't call the police. I called 9-1-1."

"That's right! And don't you ever do that again while you are at our house, unless the house is on fire!"

Mom sulked as she went off to bed, and we didn't hear anything more from her for the rest of the night.

Despite recurring incidents regarding the men in white outfits lurking in our yard, I didn't consider Mom's hallucinations anything more than a family joke, an aberration, something to laugh about after Thanksgiving dinner, when telling family stories with my brothers and their family members. I didn't know then what I learned later, that what we were dealing with were the beginning signs of dementia.

Chapter 2

RECOGNIZING
THE ENEMY

"Dementia? What in the world is dementia?" I asked my wife, Lisa, upon her return from my mom's first doctor's appointment in Tennessee.

I had never paid much attention to dementia, and my ignorance is now embarrassing. I confess I didn't even know what dementia was and, frankly, had little motivation to learn about it. For some reason, the term itself was even repulsive to me. All these "new" diseases baffled me. Alzheimer's? Didn't Ronald Reagan suffer with that during the last few years of his life? Parkinson's disease? Billy Graham and Michael J. Fox have endured that, haven't they? And ALS—Lou Gehrig's disease? The only thing I knew about that one was that I assumed Lou Gehrig had been one of its victims.

You may have heard the term *dementia* used almost in a derogatory fashion, as though the person thus described is somehow weird, dangerous, or perverted (perhaps a throwback to when dementias were associated with the final stages of syphilis). Dementia means nothing of the sort; nor does dementia mean "crazy." The term *dementia* derives from two Latin words meaning "away" and "mind," and that is probably the simplest definition of dementia—the person with the disease has suffered a loss or an impairment of his or her mental abilities. Part of the mind has gone away and will not return.

Dementia can strike anyone—rich or poor—regardless of race, environment, or education. Brilliant people and dull individuals can be afflicted, upbeat personalities or droll, people from "bad" families and "good" families, from all walks of life. There is no reason to be embarrassed if someone in your family has developed the disease.

Dementia takes various forms, the most familiar being Alzheimer's disease, which is irreversible and for which no cure is currently available. Vascular dementia is the second most widely mentioned form of the disease, which is also irreversible but doesn't seem to progress as rapidly, and for which some measure of help is available to assist the person and his or her family to better deal with the disease. Though similar in the end result, Alzheimer's disease seems to progress in a direct downhill slide, whereas vascular dementia progresses more in steps, with the patient often remaining on a step for quite a while before dropping suddenly, then remaining on that step for a season until something precipitates another noticeable decline. Sometimes a vascular dementia patient may even appear to be temporarily improving, functioning relatively close to normal. But then something might happen—a fall, or a dispute with a family member, or some other incident—and the vascular dementia patient will drop several steps.

The cause of these diseases has been widely debated, but has not been definitively agreed upon by the medical community. In my mom's situation, the doctors believed that a series of transient ischemic attacks (TIAs), commonly known as mini-strokes, wiped out her short-term memory capabilities. While she was able to vividly recall events that happened several decades ago, the mini-strokes destroyed enough of her brain tissue to affect her short-term memory and other intellectual functions to the point that often she couldn't remember what she had eaten for breakfast. Certainly, a slight forgetfulness can be common as we age, but such memory loss does not normally interfere with our daily lives. Many elderly people function actively into their seventies, eighties, and nineties. Billy Graham preached strong messages well into his eighties; astronaut Buzz Aldrin was still taking zero-gravity flights in his late seventies and performed on television's *Dancing With the Stars* at eighty years of age; Senator Bob Dole was severely wounded in World War II, but continued to be active on the American political scene as an octogenarian. My mom was still driving a car in busy Orlando traffic into her early eighties.

But then the dementia struck. Because a person with a mild case of dementia is usually able to continue doing most of what he or she has always done, the disease may not be recognized right away, or the person's actions are rationalized or excused. "Mom's always been a bit quirky anyhow," my family members and I said. "She is getting older, after all." We simply attributed Mom's sometimes-odd behavior to loneliness, tiredness, or boredom. At first it was frustrating for family members as we tried to communicate with her; then it was baffling, and eventually most people close to Mom simply gave up trying to make sense of her rude comments and erratic, inexplicable actions. Either that, or because they didn't realize the monster with which they were dealing, they became offended, put off, and simply avoided or ignored Mom as much as possible.

Sometimes the changes caused by dementia are drastic and easily discernable. The afflicted person may experience unusual changes in mood or energy levels; they may become passive, fearful, irritable, or uncharacteristically demanding. Some people with dementia or Alzheimer's experience hallucinations, often seeing, hearing, or even smelling things that just aren't there. When my mom started seeing men in white suits out in our front yard at night, I didn't realize that it was the disease talking. I didn't know she had dementia. I did recognize that, whether I could explain it or not, her hallucinations were real to her. She really thought she saw people in our yard, and it scared the daylights out of her. At that point it was silly to argue over whether or not anyone was actually looking in our windows. The best thing I could do was to agree that she was seeing them, but to assure her on the basis of my track record of truthfulness that we were not in danger.

Some people with dementia develop a habit of hiding things; they become suspicious of other people, often accusing them of stealing personal items. My mom did that constantly; she'd hide her purse, or her driver's license, couldn't find them, and then declare that someone had stolen them. We thought it was part of her personality changing, or that she was growing afraid of living alone. She often misplaced items, or couldn't remember that she even had them. I can't even begin to count how many times she lost her cell phone in her condominium.

Perhaps more disheartening was Mom's inability to control her urination or her bowel movements. At first we thought it was a bladder problem, but we later discovered that physically she was fine. She just couldn't remember to go to the bathroom in time to prevent "accidents."

With some dementia victims, these and other symptoms happen almost overnight. With other individuals, the disease conquers the human body and spirit gradually, imperceptibly. If you know the signs of Alzheimer's, you may pick up on them and secure help right away. Otherwise, you are more likely to see the early indicators only in retrospect. You may look back and be able to pin-point a particular incident where you can say, "After that occurred, Mom was never the same."

In my mom's case, something significant happened when she suffered a series of mini-strokes. A stroke occurs when blood flow and oxygen to the brain are interrupted, and, if not repaired quickly, this lack of blood flow can result in that part of the brain being permanently destroyed. When someone is having a stroke, time is of the essence. If the blood flow interruption is caused by a clot in a blood vessel to the brain, the clot can be dissolved with clot-busting drugs if the person receives treatment within a few hours. If the interruption is due to a break in a blood vessel, hem-orrhaging into the brain is far more serious. Some general signs of stroke include numbness in the face, arm, or leg—usually on one side of the body. Speech and vision problems, severe headaches, shortness of breath, unusual dizziness, or fainting may also be signs of a stroke.

Strokes are caused by a variety of conditions, including high blood pressure and high cholesterol, and can also be caused by being overweight or leading a sedentary lifestyle and not getting enough exercise. Mom had all of those factors going against her, plus one of which we were not aware until she was hospitalized. There the doctors discovered an atrial fibrillation, an abnormal heart rhythm that caused her heart to quiver slightly, hinder-ing the movement of blood between the heart's chambers and enhancing the possibility of a blood clot moving from her heart to her brain.

Mom was living on her own, so when the mini-stroke occurred, my family didn't know the specific symptoms she had experienced, even though we pressed her for information. "Oh, I don't know." She waved us off. "I wasn't feeling well, so I went next door to see the doctor, and he sent me to the hospital." Nor did we recognize the seriousness of Mom's condition at the time. After a few days of bed rest, she literally hopped out of bed and carried on with her life as though nothing had happened. And, as far as we knew, nothing had. But, unbeknownst to our family, the Mom we knew had left the building.

Chapter 3

THE MOM I USED
TO KNOW

To better understand how subtly yet severely this disease can impact a person before you recognize it, you should know a bit about how my mom lived before the dementia robbed her of her self-sufficiency.

Minnie Abraham was born October 7, 1922, in Clymer, Pennsylvania, a small coal-mining town of fewer than three thousand inhabitants—including dogs, cats, chickens, in-laws, and outlaws—and that census was probably taken on a day when everyone was hosting their family reunions. Minnie's father had been blinded in World War I after being struck by mortar shrapnel. The same explosion blew three fingers off his right hand and severely disfigured his other fingers, so Minnie never felt the soft touch of her father's hand on her face. She did, however, feel his hot breath on her collar many times, as her father compensated for his lost eyesight by running a strictly regimented family of five girls and one boy. Receiving only a minimal military pension, Minnie's family survived the Great Depression by taking odd jobs wherever they could. Minnie's mother took in washing to earn enough money to keep food on the table.

As a young woman, Minnie served our nation during World War II by working at an airplane factory. Following the war she met Howard Abraham, a handsome, dark-haired hometown boy. Howard had just returned from Okinawa, and was sauntering down the street with several buddies when he saw the attractive brunette on the sidewalk.

"Come here, little girl," the confident vet called to Minnie. "I'm going to change your name!"

And he did. They were married on October 6, 1946, had four children, all boys—John, Howard, Jr., and me. Jimmy, our fourth brother, died of pneumonia at eighteen months of age. Jimmy's death drove Mom to her knees in repentance, seeking a fresh start with God.

Mom was an independent soul, boldly going where few people had gone before. For instance, one snowy winter night she was taking some kids from our church youth group to a countywide rally. She came upon a roadblock with a large sign on it: Stop! Danger.

Most people would have turned around and found a different route. Not Mom. "I'm sorry, kids, but this is the only road I know, so we're going for it, " she explained to the carload of junior high teens. She put the car in gear and drove around the barricade and on down the road. "Alright, Mrs. A!" my friends cheered. Suddenly, I had the coolest mom in town.

The surface seemed unusually slippery, but Mom carefully negotiated her way through the darkness toward a light about a mile or two away. Something seemed amiss, though; when we arrived at the farmhouse from where the light was shining, Mom couldn't find the road to take us to the rally.

"I'll just be a minute," she said. "I'm going to stop here for some directions."

She drove up toward the back porch of the farmhouse, and as she did, an elderly man carrying a flashlight came out on the porch and headed toward our car; he had a look of sheer terror on his face. Mom rolled down the window as the man reached the car.

"Lady, where did you come from?" he asked.

"Right there, the road coming from the Brush Valley area," Mom replied, pointing back over her shoulder.

The man's mouth dropped wide open.

"That's impossible," he said. "The road has been closed since last summer, and there's now a lake covering the land where the road used to be!"

"I don't know about that," Mom replied, with a bunch of us kids sniggering in the backseat. "But we just came across the old road from Brush Valley."

The old man was awestruck. "Well, then, you just drove about a mile or two across a frozen lake!"

Mom didn't think much of it, but simply asked for directions to the town where the youth rally was to be held that night. The farmer was happy to oblige, and we went on our way, arriving late, but safe and sound. We followed friends home a different route.

The following day Mom asked some people about the new lake in what was now known as Yellow Creek State Park. Sure enough, the road was underwater. We had traversed the frozen lake in a car loaded with kids. For years we teased Mom about that slippery ride, but she took that kind of stuff in stride.

Mom played the piano in our local church, a small congregation of about eighty people. She could read music, but she preferred playing "by ear," hearing the tune and then picking it out on the keyboard, without regarding the music. It was a delight to watch her play for congregational singing with such unabashed joy. Often Mom's piano playing was louder than the entire congregation's attempt to sing the hymns, but most song leaders or pastors didn't mind. They relished Mom's vibrant, passionate approach to the hymns, even if she overshadowed the stodgy, gray-haired congregation struggling to keep up with her.

Dad played trumpet and just about any other instrument he picked up, so it was only natural that the Abraham boys should inherit some musical ability. When my brothers and I became Christians, we formed a gospel band, traveling the country in a customized motor coach, and Mom came along. Everywhere we went, as soon as our bus pulled into town, people came knocking at the door. They weren't fans hoping to get an autograph from one of the guys in the band. No, they were people looking for Mom, so she could encourage them and pray with them.

Minnie and the band.

As our music became more contemporary, our younger brother Howard, "Tink," as we called him, took over the keyboard responsibilities and Mom moved to a synthesizer, providing lush string arrangements. During some songs, she simply sang, shouted, or waved her hands high in the air, praising God. She was a show in her own right, and audiences adored her and enjoyed her uninhibited worship.

Almost every night, long after the concert had concluded, Mom would still be praying with a mom or dad whose children had turned their backs on God and were living wayward lives, or a woman in tears whose husband was not a Christian. Mom commiserated with each person, offering advice and encouragement.

"Honey, don't you give up on that man," she'd tell a woman she had met only a few minutes before. "The Bible promises that if we believe in the Lord Jesus, He will save us and our household."

All the while, her own husband was not a believer, but Mom refused to give up on our dad. She prayed for him for more than thirty-eight years, that he would come to trust in Jesus. And one night, at our concert in Trafford, Pennsylvania, a suburb of Pittsburgh, he did.

At night, when the other guys got too tired to drive, Mom sometimes slipped in behind the wheel of the forty-foot bus and drove for hours on the interstate without us boys even realizing it. When one of us awakened and walked up to the front of the bus, we'd be astonished to see the diminutive woman behind the huge steering wheel.

"Mom! You can't be driving. You need a special license to drive a bus."

"Nonsense," she'd reply. "I taught you to drive, didn't I?"

When the group got off the road after nearly twenty years, my brothers and their families moved to Florida, and I moved my family to Nashville. Mom remained in Clymer, Pennsylvania, happy to be able to spend time with my dad. They attended church together regularly, and my former bartending dad became a Sunday school teacher and an elder in the church. In many ways, he was a new person, and he and Mom were happier than ever.

They had more time to pour themselves into Little League baseball, something they had loved since my brothers and I were kids. In honor of his more than forty years of serving variously as secretary, treasurer, or president of the organization, our hometown renamed the ballpark "Hub Field," after my dad. In 1990, Mom and Dad were finally able to attend the Little League World Series in Williamsport, Pennsylvania, fulfilling one of their lifelong dreams. As they watched the games, they sat on the grass behind the center field fence and held hands like two teenagers in love.

Minnie and Hub . . . like two teenagers in love.

Chapter 4

ONE IS THE LONELIEST NUMBER

Hub and Minnie Abraham remained married for more than fifty years, until the morning of March 12, 1997, when Mom came downstairs at five a.m. and found my dad slouched in a chair. He had just gulped down his morning coffee and was ready to go to work when he suffered a massive heart attack. Mom called 9-1-1, but by the time the paramedics arrived, Dad's heart had stopped beating.

Mom called me shortly after five. Any time the telephone rings that early in the morning, most people are tempted to think the worst. *Something awful must have happened; otherwise, why is somebody calling me at this hour?* So perhaps I steeled myself for Mom's news before I picked up the phone. Through her tears, I managed to hear her say, "Ken, Daddy's gone. Your dad died a few minutes ago."

Although the words of her message floored me, I forced myself to maintain my composure to avoid sending Mom into hysteria. I talked with her briefly, and assured her that I'd be on a plane as soon as possible. Then I went into the shower, turned it on full blast, and leaned my head against the glass as my tears mixed with the water streaming down my face. Dad was only seventy-two years old.

Arranging the funeral was a blur. My brothers and I, along with my mom, met with the funeral director to choose a casket and the many other details that one rarely thinks about—or wants to think about, for that matter. I am a strong advocate of preparing for death ahead of time so grief-stricken family members are not as easily taken advantage of by funeral directors who give the appearance of concern and compassion, but are more interested in making as much money from a loved one's death as possible. Unfortunately, we hadn't done that for our dad.

The funeral director droned through his spiel. "You can have this casket over here, or that one over there" (which, of course, was three times the price of the first). We went through the same procedure for choosing the flowers, the programs, and the vault in which the casket was to finally reside, every little detail racking up the bill.

The viewing and service were sad but glorious, with several thousand people filing through the funeral home and church to pay their respects to Dad and to offer their loving condolences to Mom and our family. After the funeral, we brothers spent a few days cleaning out Dad's closets, going through his desk, and trying to alleviate as much emotional pain as possible for Mom. Tink went through all of Mom's bills, and made a file for her so she could know what needed to be paid and when. Mom and Dad owned their home and it was paid in full, as were their cars, so ostensibly she would have no problem handling monthly bills. But Mom had never managed any of the financial aspects of their life; she had rarely even written a check. Dad had done it all.

She had always been a strong, hardworking woman, so we weren't concerned about her surviving; we did wonder how well she would care for herself physically and emotionally. We had seen too many retired folks, widows and widowers who couldn't find a reason for living following the death of a spouse, deteriorate quickly. So we were glad that Mom had taken a job as a "greeter" at Wal-Mart shortly before Dad died. The irony of the fact was not lost on my brothers and me that our parents were once highly esteemed members of the local business community. Now Mom was working in a mundane occupation that evoked little respect and no small amount of ridicule.

While we had nothing but good things to say about Wal-Mart and its employees, it hurt our pride a little that Mom felt she needed to work there. Nevertheless, the job was a tremendous blessing. Working outside her home not only provided a meager income; it gave Mom a reason to get out of bed each morning. The job also expanded Mom's already large network of friends, endearing her to both customers and her fellow Wal-Mart "associates." She looked good in her blue Wal-Mart apron, and she hugged nearly everyone who came in the store. "Hi, honey, so good to see you!" She won several "Employee of the Month" and "Employee of the Year" awards.

Still, we worried about her driving to work by herself every morning, especially in winter months when western Pennsylvania was often covered with snow and ice. Mom didn't mind the weather. She got up at four a.m. to traverse the twelve miles over the undulating roads between her home and her workplace, often cutting the first swath through the freshly fallen snow. We purchased a cellular telephone Mom could keep with her in the car in case she needed help, and for several years, she functioned well on her own.

She never complained about going to work. Coming home to a quiet, empty house, however, caused her deep chagrin. Mom hated being alone. She stayed connected to her friends in the community, and especially to her church family, the same small congregation with whom she had worshipped most of her lifetime. Mom still played piano in the church, though after Dad died, she didn't play as often. Not that she was unwilling—but while she was away for a few months, a new, younger pianist had joined the church, and Mom was no longer the sought-after, premier musician.

She was lonely, of course, but each of her boys journeyed to Pennsylvania with our families as often as possible to visit her. Mom especially loved seeing her grandchildren. She was fine while we were there, but it was heart-wrenching when we prepared to leave. Tears always streamed down Mom's face while she stood on the porch and waved good-bye to us as we pulled away from the curb in front of her house. I hated leaving her like that, but our lives were in Tennessee, and Mom wanted to stay in Pennsylvania. That's where her friends were; she knew her neighbors and they all knew her.

After a while the loneliness got the best of her. We talked with her about moving to Florida if we could find her a safe, affordable environment in which to live. Eventually she agreed to a trial run, so we rented her a lovely two-bedroom apartment within a short driving distance of a Wal-Mart. We moved Mom to Florida, but kept her house in Pennsylvania—just in case. She took a job at Wal-Mart, and for more than a year did fairly well living on her own. Then she decided she wanted to move back to Pennsylvania, so we moved her home. We were back to square one.

My family moved to a different part of Nashville in 2002, and Mom visited us in our new home over Christmas. The day after Christmas, Mom sat around the kitchen table and talked with us for a while, but before long, she grew bored. She found some Windex and paper towels and busied herself cleaning the outside of our windows. I cracked up laughing. Mom rarely cleaned her own windows, even in the summertime, yet here she was cleaning ours in the middle of the winter! It was part of her personality, though, to be working. She was not content to merely sit around.

Mom was a skillful typist, accurately typing ninety words per minute, and she was tremendous at transcribing many of the interviews I did with my clients for their books. Mom took ownership of the projects too, becoming acquainted with the high-profile celebrities and news makers with whom I worked through their own words on the interview tapes I trusted her to transcribe. That created some awkward moments when my "proud mama" actually met some of my clients.

In the mid-1990s I had written a book with professional golfer Paul Azinger, a PGA Champion and cancer survivor who captained America's winning Ryder Cup team in 2010. A few years after Paul's book was published, I made the mistake of taking Mom to a professional golf tournament where Paul was playing. Golf decorum demands that spectators are quiet when players are on the tees and greens, and although the gallery crowds may roar after a shot, the pros attempt to remain "in a zone," avoiding conversations, not wanting to break their concentration. But Mom didn't know or care about golf decorum. All she knew was that her son had worked on Paul's book, and she had typed some of the transcripts. We were standing close to the ropes so she called out loudly to Paul as he was striding from the green to the next tee, "Paul. Paul Azinger. It's Minnie. Minnie Abraham. My son wrote your book! And I typed it!"

Gracious gentleman that he is, Paul stopped midstride and came to the ropes and gave Mom a hug. Unfortunately he went to the next tee and hit a horrible shot.

"That's okay, honey," Mom called out to him. "You'll do better next time."

Mom was equally as enthusiastic about my brothers' music. As if I hadn't learned anything from the Azinger incident, in the late 1990s I took Mom to an LPGA tournament, where singers Amy Grant and Vince Gill were playing in a charity round. Mom and I were standing alongside the fairway when Mom recognized Amy. Before I realized what she was doing, she had flagged down Amy as she moved from the tee up the fairway.

"Amy! Amy," Mom called out, motioning for her to come over. Perhaps because of Amy's kindness, or her great respect for her own mother, Amy dutifully edged toward the side of the fairway. "Amy Grant, I'm Minnie Abraham. You sang on my sons' album!" Mom instinctively hugged Amy.

Amy smiled warmly at Mom. "I did?"

And she had—nearly fifteen years earlier, when Amy was still in her teens, music producer Brown Bannister had asked Amy to sing a cameo background vocal on a song featuring my brother Tink. Amy probably didn't even remember the project, but Mom never forgot.

By 2003 many of my parents' friends had passed away, and the loneliness again threatened to drain the life out of my mom. Her normally bright green eyes had dulled to a grayish hazel, and her once naturally wavy dark hair had turned silver gray, with occasional specks of brunette peeking through. Her quick smile was still there, and her eyes still twinkled when talking about one of her boys, but tears dotted her cheeks much more frequently.

We decided to move Mom back to Florida, where my brother John and his wife, Sandie, owned a condominium in which Mom could live. This time, however, Mom's move would be final. She would not be returning to Pennsylvania until we flew her home for burial, which we hoped would not be any time soon.

Chapter 5

MOVING OUT,
MOVING IN

Moving Mom out of the old homestead was tough. On every bookshelf, in every drawer, we found keepsakes, pictures, and other items of sentimental value. So many precious memories washed over us, reminders of our youth and Mom's life with my dad and all that they had experienced together.

We spent several days packing up Mom's belongings, knowing that she would never be returning to live there again. Most of her heavy furniture we gave away, including her precious piano, an old upright that weighed a ton. Clothes we took by the bagful to the Salvation Army, and we filled a huge Dumpster in the backyard with outdated canned food, furniture, and other furnishings for which she would not have enough space in her condo in Florida. Our paternal grandfather had come from Syria to America in the early 1920s, entering the country through Ellis Island with nothing more than his clothing. Through sacrifice and hard work, he built a life in our little town, and the Abraham family prospered. Now Mom was leaving her hometown with little more than what our grandfather owned initially. It was the end of an era for our family.

Tink stayed behind and drove the last remnants of Mom's belongings to Florida. Mom traveled with Tink in the truck, and throughout the eighteen-hour trip repeatedly offered, "I'll be glad to drive, Tink. You need a rest."

We set up Mom in the condo, moved in all her clothes and some furniture, and bought her a large new television set for her living room. We hung family photos and pieces of inexpensive art on the wall, and set out other knickknacks, and before long, the condo looked a lot like home to Mom.

Getting reestablished in Florida was tougher this time because Mom was no longer employed. Instead she lived alone and passed the time watching television, with my brothers and their families looking in on her as often as possible. But life in Florida was different now from when Mom had visited previously. Before, when Mom traveled to Florida and stayed a few weeks during the winter, the other family members' activities revolved around her visit. It was a perpetual party, going out for dinner, visiting the many attractions in Orlando, or just attending church and being together for lunch or to watch a football game. Once Mom was a resident, however, the party was basically over. My brothers and their families had to deal with real life—which included jobs, school, lawn care, laundry, and life's myriad mundane details, all of which took time that previously had been spent with Mom. Before long, she was complaining that she was lonely again, even though my brothers and their families lived within ten minutes of her doorstep and visited her frequently.

"I never see anyone anymore," she told me when I talked with her by phone. I couldn't imagine that my brothers and their family members weren't looking in on Mom. I assumed that no matter how often my brothers stopped to see my mom, it wouldn't be nearly as often as she would prefer. It never crossed my mind that perhaps they were in fact visiting her, and Mom couldn't remember that they had been there, that she was having increasing difficulty accurately recalling any recent events.

She grew bored easily and complained incessantly that she wanted to find a job, any job, and she would too—if she only had a car. She might have been able to handle working at nearly eighty years of age, but we were concerned about her driving in the Orlando traffic. Although we didn't know it at the time, looking back, it's easy to assume that the beginning stages of dementia were already slowing her reflexes and impairing her ability to drive safely. When we moved Mom to Florida the second time, we gave away her car—perhaps providentially, but much to her chagrin. Consequently, Mom had no way of getting around except public transportation, which she hated. I couldn't blame her. The buses were hot, smelly, and crowded, with the majority of passengers speaking languages my mom had never heard, much less understood, so she was more than a little nervous when she attempted to negotiate the city aboard public transportation. I wonder now if she was afraid to board the buses, perhaps unable to remember where to get off, or confused about which bus to take, or even the direction in which she was going. Whatever the reason, Mom shied away from riding the bus. Besides, Mom was convinced that she could still drive. Her new mantra, "If I only had a car . . ." became a favorite joke in our family.

Separating a loved one with dementia from his or her automobile is no small feat. Most seniors want to continue driving long after they are mentally safe to do so. Getting them to give up the car keys is often perceived as tantamount to taking away their freedom. Mom wanted her car so she could get another job, drive to the grocery store or drugstore on her own, or visit her sister Ruth, who lived only a few miles away and was bedfast. What hard-hearted person could refuse such a request? One who loved her, that's who.

Driving, of course, is a learned activity and becomes almost automatic for most of us. But it is a skill that requires a great deal of interaction between the brain, eyes, hands, and feet, not to mention the ability to analyze and adapt quickly to myriad potentially dangerous situations. In Mom's case, all of her responses seemed to be slowing down. She admitted, "I'm not as sharp as I used to be, but I can still drive a car better than you boys. Don't forget, I'm the one who taught you to drive." But we realized that even if Mom was physically able to operate a vehicle, she might endanger the life of somebody else. As tough a choice as it was, we refused to allow her to drive. Turns out, that was the right call, but I'm not sure Mom ever forgave us for that!

My brothers or their wives made a special effort to be available any time Mom needed to go to the grocery store; they or one of our nephews were always glad to take her. But being dependent on others to get around was a new experience for Mom, and not one she preferred.

Moreover, Mom had precious little money. With her only income around $700 per month from Social Security, Mom could afford few luxuries after her rent was paid. The good news? She didn't need much. If she had enough money for food, candy, and a few Christmas and birthday gifts for her children and grandchildren, she was happy and content.

The family members in Florida did their best to keep Mom active and involved in church. One of my brothers or my nephew Marc picked Mom up and took her to Sunday school and church each Sunday. She reluctantly attended a senior adult class, griping that she just knew she wouldn't like it, but when she got into the class, she noticed a piano, and glory be! The class needed a piano player! Mom became the regular pianist for that class of senior adults and they welcomed her each week.

After church my brothers and their families took Mom out to eat, and during football season, they gathered together weekly, usually at a Buffalo Wild Wings restaurant with multiple television screens where they could watch Mom's favorite team—the Pittsburgh Steelers. She and grandson Marc stayed long after the other family members went home, sometimes until seven o'clock in the evening, watching various games. Mom loved football, but more importantly, she was elated to be with her family. It really didn't take much to make Mom happy.

Chapter 6

PARANOIA AND
SUSPICIONS

Living alone, Mom had plenty of time to clean her Florida condo, but more often than not, her living space was in disarray and cluttered. She often left food out on the countertops in the kitchen. We thought she was just messy. Now we realize that she simply forgot where things were supposed to be stored, or possibly even forgot that she had gotten them out in the first place. But she never forgot to lock her doors.

Alzheimer's studies indicate that people with dementia seem to recall incidents from the past that they associate with strong emotions, either good or bad. Mom had a habit of blocking her front door with chairs because she was afraid somebody was trying to break in all the time. I often wondered if she had been sexually assaulted as a young girl because she constantly worried that some man "was trying to get in her pants." My brothers and I teased her,

"Mom, you're eighty-some years old. Any guy who tries to get into those pants would be risking his life!"

"It's not funny!" Mom retorted. "I know when somebody is looking at me that way." Indeed, the last couple of years that she lived in Florida on her own, she seemed always to be living in fear. Frequently she fretted that intruders were climbing onto her air-conditioning unit, trying to break into her condo. My brother John jokingly told her, "Mom, open the door and let them come in! You don't have anything of value that any burglar would want."

That, of course, was the wrong answer and no consolation to Mom. Since we didn't know that Mom had dementia, we dismissed her fear as unfounded paranoia. "That's just Mom," we said. "She's always been afraid of her own shadow." But had we thought about it, that really wasn't the case. She had always been an independent, courageous woman. And had we known the symptoms of dementia, we might have realized that her unwarranted fears were early indicators that something was seriously wrong.

Mom called the police so frequently she was on a first-name basis with the 9-1-1 operators. The local police officers responded immediately at first; after a while, they simply called my brother, saying, "John, your mother called again." Finally they stopped going to her home at all when she called.

Mom worried constantly that someone would attempt to steal something from her. Tink bought her a portable electronic piano and delivered it to her condo so she could play the old hymns she loved so much. He helped her set up the keyboard in her spare bedroom. Mom profusely thanked Tink and his family for the piano. But as soon as they left, she took it down off its stand and returned it to the box because she feared someone might see it and want to steal the keyboard. Similarly, she brought her patio furniture inside her apartment and put it in her living room each night. "Somebody might steal it if I leave it outside."

We didn't realize that Mom's paranoia was attributable to a growing dementia, that individuals with dementia frequently think that somebody is trying to harm them or steal from them, even when no threats exists. We simply thought Mom was being unreasonable. But no amount of assurances of her safety eased her mind. Mom continued to carry the outdoor furniture inside every night.

We now know that a person with dementia may misinterpret seemingly innocuous information as a threat. If Mom saw or heard the news about a robbery somewhere in Orlando, she assumed that the thieves would be breaking into her apartment next. Providing factual information rarely helped allay her concerns.

"Mom, that break-in was almost an hour from where you live. You are snug as a bug in a rug."

She'd smile and say, "That's good." But she still brought in the outdoor furniture that night.

Just because a loved one is failing doesn't mean that he or she is totally clueless. Don't ignore their complaints. Mom often had kernels of truth mixed in with some of the nutty things she'd say. One night there actually was a prowler outside her back door and apparently up to no good. John discovered a man's footprint on top of the condo's air-conditioning unit, located inside Mom's patio fence. When Mom saw the print, she responded with a cross between jubilance and terror.

"See! I told you someone was trying to break in!" She found a large metal rod and placed it in the grooved track behind the glass sliding door. "There, that will keep him out," she declared confidently.

Chapter 7

THAT DOESN'T EVEN SOUND LIKE GRANDMA!

S ome elderly people become belligerent as they move into Alzheimer's and dementia, exhibiting signs of unreasonable stubbornness, impulsiveness, or extremely quirky behavior. We'd heard stories of good, godly people turning into profanity-spewing, self-absorbed narcissists due to dementia. One of my favorite college professors, a preacher who positively influenced thousands of young men and women, developed Alzheimer's in his later years. A man who ordinarily would have been offended at words and phrases such as "doggone" or "holy mackerel" suddenly became a toilet mouth. At first his language was shocking to the family, then it became almost funny since it was so out of character for him, and then it became embarrassing as he repeatedly offended visitors who didn't understand it was the disease speaking, not their long-standing friend and godly mentor.

I'd also heard of instances where Alzheimer's or dementia caused a kind, gentle, polite person to become extremely aggressive. One ninety-year-old man grabbed the gearshift of his daughter's car as she was driving him to a doctor's appointment. He jerked the gearshift out of position, resulting in an earsplitting grinding noise, and nearly causing an accident. The normally docile father had responded in fear and confusion because he didn't know where he was or who was driving the car.

Another woman's mother violently snatched a gold necklace from her granddaughter's neck, cutting into her skin. "It's mine! Give it back," the grandmother with dementia demanded. The sweet, demure granny let loose a series of expletives, calling her granddaughter every name in the book, the nicest being "a thief." The mother and granddaughter left in tears, the granddaughter vowing never to visit again.

Caregivers who work with Alzheimer's and dementia patients have noted some common causes for these outbursts: overexertion, confusion, or too much excitement or stimulation; they've also observed frequent aggressive behavior late in the day, a pattern professional caregivers refer to as "sundowning." It was helpful for us to learn that we couldn't and shouldn't argue with Mom or try to reason with her when she said or did irrational things. Instead we simply changed the activity or the subject of conversation and that usually calmed her down.

In the earliest stages of Mom's dementia, even before we knew what was going on, Mom sometimes showed signs of losing a sense of decorum. Our daughters always loved to hear Grandma Minnie's stories about the good old days, or even the difficult days of living through the Great Depression, or how America responded to World War II. The girls listened, mesmerized by Mom's colorful tales. But one day, even before Mom was diagnosed with dementia, she began telling our teenage daughters sordid stories of her years in Baltimore working in a factory helping to build airplanes. "We'd go out and get so drunk after work, I'd wake up in somebody's car and not even know the person," she admitted.

"Grandma!" The girls would recoil in horror at thoughts of their godly, Bible-toting, Christian matriarch of the family living such a profligate lifestyle.

"Oh, yes, we used to drink grain alcohol mixed with orange juice and it would put us under the table in a few minutes." Mom went on to describe some of her sexual exploits in specific detail.

"Grandma!"

"Hey, Mom, let's go get some ice cream," I interrupted when I realized where the conversation was going.

"Oh, yes! Ice cream would be wonderful!" Mom answered. "But you girls just remember that a boy only has one thing on his mind—"

"Ice cream," I said, waving at the girls to head to the car.

I didn't know it at the time, but the loss of the "filters" regarding appropriateness is another common symptom of dementia. I merely thought Mom was being too open with her conversation, as some elderly folks are prone to be.

She did something similar with Greg, Lisa's hairstylist, when we took Mom to get her hair done. While Greg styled her hair, Mom entertained him with all sorts of outlandish stories about her experiences in Baltimore, enough to make anyone blush. Greg, an interesting character in his own right, loved every titillating detail, laughing along with my mom, gasping frequently in feigned shock, as though he just couldn't believe that a conservative Christian woman would do such things. Greg's response spurred Mom's storytelling even more. Meanwhile Lisa sat, red-faced embarrassed, in a chair across the room.

Despite his playful attitude with Mom, Greg recognized her decline since the last time he'd styled her hair. He later confided to Lisa, "Something has happened to Minnie. She's different; she seems to be slipping."

Mom never became aggressively mean and nasty, and since she was already quirky, we didn't notice much difference in her conversation—at first. But, more and more, we recognized that her "filters" were gone. She'd say things that were rude, hurtful, or sometimes even profane. Not often, but occasionally, she'd let out a blue streak of expletives that would make a sailor blush. "Wow!" one of our daughters said when she heard Mom slip. "That doesn't even sound like Grandma Minnie!"

Mostly, though, Mom simply said things that were insensitive, never intentionally insulting but cutting nonetheless. We now realize that it was not "Mom" doing the speaking, but the filters of common decency and respect being bypassed by the dementia.

We quickly discovered, however, that it was of no use in trying to correct her irrational behavior or to offer gentle reproofs for such improper outbursts. We learned to go with the flow. Half the time she wasn't even aware that she had said anything wrong, and clearly she meant no harm. If I pointed out that she had said something amiss, or expressed disappointment about something she had spoken, she adamantly protested, "Ken, I would never say such a thing."

"Ah, you just did, Mom."

"No, I did not. You must have heard me wrong. Clean out your ears."

Mom cooked sparingly, rarely making herself a real meal; instead she ate a lot of junk food, especially sugar-filled snacks. People with dementia and Alzheimer's are particularly fond of sweets. Mom was always up for another piece of candy, a large piece of cake or pie, or some ice cream. Oddly enough, she was actually losing weight, probably due to her poor nutritional habits. Rather than cooking, she'd open a bag of cookies and eat the entire contents as a meal. Ironically, she once was a wonderful cook. Anytime her boys were home, she put on a spread as though she were feeding an army. Now she went to the grocery store with my brothers or sisters-in-law and grabbed three or four of each item.

"Mom, why are you getting four bags of potatoes?" my brother asked.

"Because I might need them, and I don't know when I might get back to the grocery store again." Of course, now we know that hoarding is one of the favorite pastimes of people with dementia, but at the time, her unreasonable behavior simply irritated my brothers and their wives. Our daughters, however, saw the humor in their grandmother's excesses, and coined the phrase regarding her shopping habits: "If one is good, ten are better!"

Mom was always writing checks to family members—none of which we ever cashed—for birthdays, anniversaries, or holidays. In her younger years, she never missed buying cards and presents for everyone, but now she usually didn't remember to send anything until someone reminded her that a member of the family was celebrating a special occasion. Mom would hurry and dash off a check and put it in the mail. We always received her gifts with great gratitude, but she really had no money to spare, so we simply thanked her and went on as though we had cashed the checks. Since Mom had never balanced a checkbook in her life, we weren't too afraid of messing up her accounting system. It was a good deal all around. Mom received the joy of giving, and we received the benefit of her kindness without draining her bank account.

When she sent a twenty-five-dollar check to our daughter, Ashleigh, for her eighteenth birthday, Ashleigh asked, "What should I do, Dad? If I cash it, she will be out that money, and if I don't cash it, she's going to know."

"Just do what you think is best," I said.

Ashleigh looked at the check as though it were written for a million dollars. To a first-year college student, twenty-five dollars was a lot of money. She smiled and put the check in her purse.

"I think I'll just hang on to this for a few years," she said.

Chapter 8

ACCIDENTS HAPPEN

In order to give my brothers and their families a break, and to provide Mom a vacation, my wife, Lisa, and I arranged frequent trips for Mom to visit us in Tennessee, especially for holidays and birthdays. Our daughter Alyssa's sixteenth birthday party was a perfect occasion for such a trip. We flew Mom in a week before the big event so she could travel along with some senior adults on a special weekend bus tour to Branson, Missouri. Mom knew Fred and Eleanor Garton and several other people on the trip who attended our Sunday school class. Fred was a truck driver by profession and he was driving the bus; we were also able to arrange a roommate for Mom, so I felt comfortable in letting her travel without us.

Mom enjoyed the gospel and country music shows in Branson, as well as the many Ozark Mountain craft shops. She did fairly well in getting around, but she and her roommate were constantly late, lost, or confused. At several points the Gartons went out of their way to find Mom and make sure she got on the bus. (Had it not been for Fred and Eleanor watching out for her, Mom might still be in Branson!) When the group returned to Nashville, Eleanor came to Lisa and me, her concern for my mom genuine and heartfelt.

"Please don't let Minnie travel alone anymore," Eleanor said. "It's not safe."

Mom, however, was happy as a lark. As far as she was concerned, the Branson trip had been a rousing success, an indication that she could do quite well on her own. Now she was looking forward to attending Alyssa's party, a swing-dance event to be held in downtown Nashville.

The party was to begin at 7:00 p.m., but we couldn't get in the building until 5:00 p.m., so we had to unload all the food, decorations, and party items right in the midst of rush-hour traffic. We worked out the details as meticulously as a commando raid, planning who would take what box out of the car in what order. But when the time came to leave for the party, Mom didn't want to go.

"I don't feel well," she said. "I'm going to lie down for a while."

"Mom! You can't lie down now. We have to go. We've timed everything precisely so we can get through the traffic and unload all the party items in time."

"You go ahead," she begged off. "Maybe I'll come later."

"How are you going to come later? You can't drive in downtown Nashville."

"I know. If I only had a car."

"No, no, no. It wouldn't make any difference if you had a car. I can't have you driving downtown. It wouldn't be safe for you or for other people."

"I'm going to lie down now," Mom said, and with that she went upstairs and crawled into bed.

What to do, what to do? I was concerned for my mom, but we had several dozen teenagers and chaperones set to show up downtown in a few hours expecting a birthday dance party. Worse yet, how embarrassing would it be for our daughter turning sixteen if we blew it on her big night? We had to get to the party, and then we'd deal with Mom and her ailments.

We left the doors to our house unlocked and headed for downtown. On the way, my wife and I racked our brains trying to think of someone we could send to our house to check on Mom. It had to be someone who knew our home, and someone who Mom might recognize enough to prevent her from calling the police again. We finally settled on Heather Stevens, a dear friend from church. We hoped that Mom might remember Heather from seeing her in our home and in Sunday school class. Heather also sang on the first row of Christ Church choir, and Mom loved listening to the choir sing. So there was a chance that, if Heather could get into the house without an incident, she could check on Mom and stay with her until we got home.

Heather took along her eighteen-year-old niece Brittney. When the women arrived at our home, they repeatedly rang the front doorbell, but nobody answered. They decided to peek their heads inside the foyer and call out Mom's name, hoping not to frighten her.

"Minnie. Minnie?" Heather called. "It's Heather from church. Are you here? Are you okay? Hello? Minnie? Where are you?"

Just then, they heard a noise emanating from one of the bedrooms, so Heather and Brittney climbed the stairs calling Mom's name softly so she wouldn't be startled when she heard them.

"Hello? Minnie?"

They found Mom in the guest room bathroom, and it was immediately obvious that she had not made it there on time. She had had an accident and was a mess. She appeared weak and pale. "Oh, Miss Minnie! Are you okay?" Heather asked.

"Oh, no, honey," Mom replied. "I'm not feeling very well. I've been sitting here for quite a while."

The women helped support Mom by her forearms, lifted her off the commode, and quickly set about washing her. Heather found a clean nightgown for Mom to wear, and they helped her to an upstairs sofa, where they gave her some water to drink. Brittney had never before met my mom, but in a matter of minutes, she and Heather and Mom were visiting like old friends.

Then, in midsentence, Mom said. "Uh, oh!" That's about as much as she could say before her entire digestive system seemed to come undone. "I have to get to the bathroom!" she cried.

Too late.

An explosion of diarrhea surged down Mom's legs. The women tried in vain to hurry Mom along to the bathroom, but everywhere she stepped, she left a trail all over our white carpet. "Oh, I'm so sorry, honey," she kept saying as the women hastened to find toilet paper and towels. Heather and Brittney had no sooner gotten Mom cleaned up and back into bed when The Attack of the Super-Accident struck again. This time, Mom didn't even make it out of bed.

By the time we arrived home, Heather and Brittney were exhausted and my mom was sleeping soundly in bed. Lisa, her sister Debbie, and I cleaned carpet and clothing, and even the walls, for quite a while into the following morning.

Shortly after dawn we heard Mom moving about in her bedroom. Thinking she might be having a relapse, I ran up the stairs to see if I could help her. To my amazement, she was up and dressed and perfectly fine.

"Good morning," she said cheerily, as though the night before had never happened. "I'm going to make some coffee and then get after those windows. Some birds pooped all over them."

"Ah, yeah, Mom. Another bird pooped all over some other places too." She didn't catch my meaning at all as she headed down to the kitchen. "Are you sure you are feeling okay?"

"Why, sure!" she replied perkily. "Never better!"

Mom stayed with us through Thanksgiving, then returned to Florida to celebrate Christmas with the family there. Getting Mom home to Florida after one of her visits to Nashville was always an adventure. She was able to walk, and enjoyed travel by air, but the long corridors of the airport were difficult for her to traverse. Although I hated seeing Mom in a wheelchair, it was much easier to procure a chair from the airlines and take her by wheelchair to her flight. She was reluctant to let a bellman assist her, so to lessen her concerns I obtained a pass from the airlines permitting me to accompany Mom through security and to take her to her gate.

It was no easy matter to negotiate airport security checks with Mom in the wheelchair, along with her purse and a large bag filled with everything from cookies to toilet paper. Besides that, it always proved daunting to get Mom in and out of the wheelchair long enough to walk through the security sensors. Worse yet, Mom had a metal plate in her foot, resulting from an accident that occurred when she had slipped on the ice and fallen off her front porch years ago and broken her ankle. Sometimes I remembered to tell the TSA officers about the plate and sometimes I didn't. But when I forgot, we lit up the alarms in a hurry.

"Oh, honey, that's nothing," Mom told the officer as he ordered her out of line, electronic wand in hand. "Don't you worry about a thing," she assured him.

Because of the many details in getting Mom through airport security, I usually allowed plenty of time when taking her to her flight. Mom was reluctant to go and wanted to spend every last minute with our family before heading back to the airport. Ordinarily, I was okay with that, since we lived less than half an hour away from Nashville International. But one evening following a holiday, we stayed a little too long at our house before getting underway. I raced to the airport and began the security marathon.

No sooner had we exited the security area, Mom turned around in her wheelchair and said, "Ken, I need to go to the bathroom."

Oh, boy. "Okay, Mom. I'll wheel you to the door of the restroom and then I'll help you up. You go on in and try to be quick. We don't have a lot of time before your plane leaves."

"Oh, you know me. I'll be quick," she replied. I wheeled Mom right into a doorless restroom entryway and helped her struggle out of the wheelchair. She shuffled into the restroom while I waited outside, trying to appear inconspicuous to the women entering and exiting the restroom.

I waited and waited. *What was taking so long?* I wondered. I stood just outside the women's restroom, looking at my watch, pacing back and forth. It's a wonder that someone didn't call security. When Mom failed to come out, I tried calling into the women's restroom entryway.

"Mom? Are you in there?" *Where else could she be?* "Are you okay?" No answer. I continued pacing back and forth outside the restroom, boldly approaching perfect strangers as they exited. "Did you happen to see a little lady in there? She was wearing a green jacket with black pants, and her flight is about to leave without her." Most of the female passengers eyed me suspiciously and said nothing. A few shook their heads and hurried toward their flights.

Finally I heard Mom calling. "Ken, I'm coming."

I glued my eyes to the restroom exit until I saw her shuffling out of the restroom, holding on to the arm of an attractive young woman.

"She couldn't get her slacks up," the woman said with a smile. "So she was stuck in the stall." Instant visions of my mom hovering above the commode trapped in her own underwear flitted through my mind. It was sad, but funny at the same time.

"We got them up though, didn't we, Minnie? She'll be fine till she gets to Florida."

As the woman hurried off to catch her flight, I marveled at the immediate rapport she and my mom shared. They had just met in the restroom stall and the woman knew Mom's name and her travel destination. That was Mom; accidents or not, she never met a person in the restroom who didn't become an instant friend.

Chapter 9

THE STRANGE URGE TO STEAL AND OTHER SIGNS WE MISSED

For a saintly woman, Mom developed a strange, insatiable urge to take things that didn't belong to her—or things she didn't need. This, too, we later learned was something often associated with dementia, and that a person with Alzheimer's may not remember what does and does not belong to him or her. Or he or she may simply not recall any reason not to take something. Shoplifting by Alzheimer's patients is common, sometimes because the person can't remember that items must be paid for before leaving the store, or maybe because he or she can't remember how the system even works. So your godly Grandpa simply walks out of the store with a new hammer, setting off all the security alarms.

Now I know that a person with dementia or Alzheimer's can

actually carry a wallet-sized card stating that he or she is memory impaired, and most stores will not press charges for minor theft, but at the time, we were clueless and often embarrassed by Mom's sudden kleptomania. When we went out to eat at a restaurant, she always came home with a pocketful of sugar or sugar substitute packs. Mom didn't even use sugar on anything, but she rationalized that somebody might need some sweetener in a cup of coffee.

For our daughter Megan's wedding, in June 2005, Lisa encouraged Mom to borrow a beautiful pearl necklace. Set against her favorite periwinkle dress—the one Mom was convinced that she had worn to her own wedding (she had actually worn the dress to Lisa's and my wedding)—the pearl necklace looked great on Mom. She looked gorgeous, though she insisted on doing her hair herself, which entailed washing her hair and letting it air-dry naturally. Not a good idea stylistically. Nevertheless, Mom enjoyed the wedding, and we were honored to have her attend. When she returned to Orlando, she took the necklace with her.

One day, a few weeks later, Lisa was looking for that necklace when we realized that my mom had not returned it. Mom had "forgotten all about it," which at the time we thought was just her way of claiming the necklace for herself. We didn't realize that two aspects of dementia were at play in this situation. The first was her honest lack of memory regarding the necklace. She probably didn't even know she had it or, if she did, she couldn't remember where she got it. The other aspect is less noble: people with dementia often get "sticky fingered," pilfering and picking up anything that is loose. We teased her about trying to steal Lisa's "priceless" necklace, which made Mom even more upset. We were joking, but in her mind, our accusations were serious. My brother Tink solved the matter when he found the necklace in Mom's condo. He made Mom send the necklace back to Lisa and gently chided her for trying to snatch it.

As dementia slowly crept in unawares, Mom's memory further degenerated, and she complained more frequently. Her normally sweet attitude turned sour, and I honestly thought that she was simply being cantankerous or ungrateful.

Part of her anxiety stemmed from the fact that the fabric of her Florida neighborhood had changed—seemingly overnight—from a semiaffluent area to a multinational community in which English was nearly a foreign language. Mom didn't mind the new complexion of the neighbors, but she was accustomed to talking freely with anyone who would stand still long enough. My brothers used to laugh at her for the way she could engage in a long, drawn-out conversation with almost anyone who called. After talking on the telephone to someone for nearly an hour, she'd hang up and smile.

"Who was that, Mom?" one of us would ask.

"I don't know," she answered honestly. "It was a wrong number."

Now, however, most of her neighbors hailed from locations outside America's borders, and Mom had difficulty bridging the language barriers. Not that she didn't try.

When I called her one day, she told me that the night before she had been out late to a Bible study with some people in her condo complex.

"Wow, that's great, Mom. I'm so glad you are getting around to meeting your new neighbors. What was the Bible study about?"

"I don't know," she said. "It was all in Spanish."

It would have been helpful had we been able to detect the early warnings of dementia developing in Mom; maybe medications could have slowed the onset of the disease. If nothing else, we would have better understood what we were dealing with.

Certainly we were aware of Mom's memory loss, but forgetting appointments or names was nothing new for her. We had teased her for years about her tendency to confuse names, from R2D2 of *Star Wars*, which she called RTDT, to mistakenly telling a famous songwriter, "You just keep writing those little songs, George." His name was Gordon.

Sure, she had difficulty tracking her monthly bills, but that wasn't new either. Inability to perform normal daily tasks, getting lost in the city, trouble finding the right word in a conversation, misplacing items, false accusations, poor judgment in dealing with money, withdrawing from friends, exhibiting moodiness, suspicion, or excessive anxiety—all of which may be indicators of Alzheimer's—were so common with Mom, we noticed nothing amiss. None of our family members had studied Alzheimer's or dementia, so we probably wouldn't have recognized most signs had they hit us in the face. Oh, sure, we recognized that Mom's mind wasn't as sharp, but we rationalized everything Mom did with the blanket excuse, "She's getting old!"

For my brother John's birthday in September 2007, his wife, Sandie, threw a gala party at their home to celebrate with dozens of friends. It was the sort of environment in which Mom normally flourished, moving from person to person in the crowd, saying things such as, "Well, hello, honey! Where have you been? I haven't seen you in ages." Or, "You need to eat more. You're getting too thin. Let me get you a piece of cake."

But not this year.

For the duration of the party, Mom sat on the corner of a couch in the television room, sullen, hardly saying a word to anyone other than family members. When Lisa or I tried to encourage her to move around the room with us, meeting new friends or greeting familiar faces, she declined.

"No, honey; I'm tired. I'm going to sit right here."

Her actions were uncharacteristic of her, but I didn't recognize that anything was wrong. I merely thought she was having a bad day.

Although Mom lived only a few minutes away from my brothers, she called their places of employment to talk with them every day. Most days she called multiple times. She didn't need anything or want anything other than to speak to them, but they were working and the line on which Mom was calling was the toll-free number she had called when she lived in Pennsylvania. The receptionists were always nice to her, but it was a problem. "John, your mother is on the phone . . . again."

"Mom, please don't call me at work unless it is an emergency," John gently chided her.

"John," she answered in a huff, "I never call you at work."

"Yes, Mom, you do. Several times. Every day. I'm always glad to hear from you, but I have to work for a living, and my boss doesn't appreciate me wasting time on the phone."

"I wouldn't think of wasting your time."

"I know, Mom. Just please don't call me at work. Call me at home or call Sandie during the day." It was a frustrating, futile effort on my brother's part, with much the same scenario played out day after day.

Not only was her mental acuity slipping, but Mom's physical body began betraying her more frequently. A strong swimmer all of her life, one day, while swimming in John and Sandie's pool, Mom sank to the bottom and couldn't get out of the water. John, Tink, and Marc dove into the pool to rescue her. Mom was insistent that something in the water was pulling her down.

"Nothing is in the pool, Mom. There's nothing to pull you down."

"Well, something did. I couldn't get away from it."

John shrugged his shoulders and left it at that. No use arguing. Mom was convinced that something had pulled her under the water.

Looking back, I can't help but wonder if she was beginning to suffer more of the short mini-strokes, which interfered with her brain enough that she couldn't move her arms and legs to swim.

One day when John stopped by to see her, she couldn't get out of bed. She had soiled her bedclothes, and the condo smelled like an outhouse. She had made another mess, similar to what she had done at our house a year earlier.

"Come on, Mom, I want you to come home with me till you feel better," John told her.

"No, no, I'm fine. Just a little loose in my stools right now," she quipped with a smile.

Despite Mom's protests, John took her home with him and Sandie put her to bed. The next day Mom couldn't get up to go to the bathroom, so she had frequent "accidents," soiling the bedding. That she didn't make it to the bathroom on time wasn't unusual, but that she didn't make it at all was something new. Again, we didn't realize what was happening, but it is possible that the mini-strokes that eventually destroyed her short-term memory had already intensified. She remained bedfast for a few days; then, without any change in her treatment or medication, a few days later she sat up, got out of bed, and went about the day as though nothing had happened. She felt fine, she declared.

Sandie thought that Mom was "playing" her, that she was merely pretending to be sick so she could get more attention from John. But, in truth, we didn't know that this was the beginning of the end.

Chapter 10

WHEN LIVING ALONE
IS NO LONGER POSSIBLE

Despite the downward trend in Mom's abilities, there were still occasions when she seemed lucid, cogent, and almost like the parent we'd always known. One of those times resulted from a serendipitous decision on Lisa's and my part to have a surprise eighty-fifth birthday party for Mom in Tennessee on October 7, 2007. But not just any party—no, this was going to be a return to Mahaffey Camp Meeting, the church camp Mom attended as a young girl. We borrowed hymnbooks from our church, decorated the house like an old camp meeting, and set out photos of Mom when she was younger. One of our friends that Mom loved, Tommy Ring, brought a Kurzweil keyboard and set it up in our living room.

"You guys are going to be so blessed for honoring your mom like this," Tommy said, as he prepared the piano.

Our plan was to let guests call out requests and have Mom play them, unrehearsed and with no advance notice, as we sang along in an old-fashioned hymn sing. We invited our Sunday school class, and were pleasantly surprised when more than eighty people showed up at our house to celebrate Mom's birthday. Our daughter Megan took Mom out to get her hair done earlier that afternoon, and kept her away from the house until we decorated and the party guests gathered. We turned off the lights in our foyer and waited. Mom was nearly at the front door when it crossed my mind that maybe her heart couldn't handle such a surprise.

Megan opened the door and Mom stepped inside. "Surprise!" Everyone yelled as we flipped on the lights, causing Mom to reel backward with a look of total shock on her face. For a moment, I feared that we'd lost her, that we had indeed induced a heart attack and she was going to topple over backward onto the front porch and roll back down the stairs. But she recovered her balance, and when she realized what was happening, she immediately began apologizing for responding negatively.

"I'm so sorry," she said to some guests. "I didn't know what was going on. Nobody told me anything!"

We presented Mom with a large bouquet of flowers, and after a full "southern style" dinner of fried chicken, green beans, mashed potatoes, and yeast rolls, we sang "Happy Birthday" and enjoyed birthday cake and ice cream. Then we gathered everyone in the family room.

"Mom, we want you to play for us, and we're going to sing along," I told her. I helped her get situated behind the Kurzweil.

"Oh, I don't know if I can play this," she said, fumbling with the controls. But the moment someone picked out a song to sing, Mom was all over the keyboard.

We sang "Amazing Grace," "Victory in Jesus," "How Great Thou Art," and dozens of other songs. Without reading the music,

"I can play as long as you can sing!"

Mom played every song by memory, and she sang every word along with us, often singing the harmony part. It was truly amazing to witness. Mom could barely remember what day it was, but she could still remember all those old hymns by heart! Additionally, Mom directed our impromptu choir from the piano, and whenever she spotted anyone not singing his or her best, she'd point and say, "Come on, honey! Sing!" Our friends responded positively and made Mom feel so special as she played and played. After an hour or so, someone asked, "Minnie, are you tired of playing?"

Mom looked shocked. "Honey, I can play as long as you can sing!" she quipped, and started into another song. We laughed and sang for more than two hours.

"Minnie, you should move to Tennessee," several friends attending the party told her.

"Well, I just might," she replied. "I'd love that."

Of course we'd thought of moving Mom to Tennessee, but we

had more family members in Florida, so it made sense for her to live there. But then Mom fell down the steps at her condo. She had slipped and fallen before, always landing on her behind and bouncing right back to her feet, but when she tumbled down the stairs all the way from upstairs to downstairs, she landed in a heap in the stairwell and couldn't get up. The phone was located across the room and she was stuck. It took her a long time to crawl to the phone and call my brothers for help. Fortunately she wasn't seriously hurt, but it did send a wake-up call to my brothers and me. Perhaps it wasn't such a good idea for Mom to live on her own any longer.

Making the decision where to place her was difficult. Did we really want to "institutionalize" our mother? She was still able to walk, to get around and take care of herself, so we preferred that she have some flexibility and mobility. But she needed other people around her. We considered live-in caregivers, but knew Mom would not accept that option. Maybe Mom might be able to live permanently with one of our families, or split time between the family members. My brothers and I conferred with our spouses, and we all decided that we wanted to remain married. Mom would have driven any of us crazy had we allowed her to move in with us. Fortunately, Mom was still healthy and able to live independently, which gave us more options. Once a senior citizen needs assistance, the options go down and the costs go up, with the costs eventually skyrocketing exponentially.

Lisa and I talked more about moving Mom to Nashville. For me, it was an easy decision. This was payback time—my mom had sacrificially cared for me as a child, and had significantly helped me in my writing career, never with any thought of a return. She didn't do it for money or recognition; she did it for love. If she lived to be a hundred, I could not repay the debt I owed her. I didn't feel that I had to take care of her; I felt honored to take care of such a marvelous woman, a woman who had gone into the shadow of death to help bring me to life, who had poured out her life for God, for other people, and yes, for me. I wasn't coerced into caring for Mom; I was privileged to give back a little to her during what were obviously going to be her final years.

Nevertheless, I could not and would not have encouraged Mom to move to Nashville had Lisa not been in full agreement. If you are looking for a good excuse to get divorced, I assure you that unilaterally inviting a senior, dependent loved one into your home is about the surest prescription for the destruction of a marriage you will ever find. While it may seem noble to make such a decision whether your spouse is in favor of it or not, if you are married, you and your spouse need to weigh the issues involved and be in absolute agreement that this is really something you want to do. If you have kids still living at home, a sincere, frank discussion of how your elderly loved one's move will affect them is only fair.

My family evaluated the issues and decided the trade-offs were worth it. I began investigating independent living facilities in Nashville. I must admit, I wasn't prepared for the sticker shock. Many of the homes were lovely, but the rent for small apartment-style living areas, with meals served in a common dining room, were outrageously high. Still, most of the independent living facilities offered a sense of community, as well as protective security and emergency call buttons in case a senior needed help, a valuable feature.

Lisa and I visited the "Manor," a relatively new independent living complex within fifteen minutes of our home. The grounds were immaculately kept, replete with beautiful flowers and neatly trimmed hedges and trees all around the property. Inside, the Manor was clean and impeccably decorated, with stylish furniture, paintings in the hallways, and a regal-looking dining room. Waiters dressed in crisply starched white shirts served the residents on beautifully appointed tables, complete with fresh tablecloths and centerpieces.

We met with Brenda, the Activities Director, who outlined the busy schedule of activities available to residents, everything from bingo to beanbag baseball to bridge tournaments to Bible studies. Additionally, Brenda regularly booked entertainers to perform at the Manor, taking residents on a musical tour down memory lane.

Considering the Manor's splendid array of food, activities, and entertainment, Lisa quipped, "It's like taking a cruise without leaving the dock!"

My brothers and I talked further about moving Mom to Nashville. Although the financial costs tripled what she was paying in Orlando, we recognized that we had to do something, that Mom could no longer live alone. She might leave the gas on in her stove, burn down the condo complex, or walk out in the middle of the street and get lost. All were now distinct possibilities.

I talked to my mom by phone almost every night, so one evening I gently suggested that we'd love to have her living in Nashville. I was almost surprised at how easily I convinced her to move, though I could tell that she worried about "what the other boys might think."

"Oh, I think everybody would be okay with you coming up here to live for a while. After all, the airlines fly both ways, and you can always go back and visit, or they can come here to visit you." I described an attractive picture of what her life in Nashville could be. The one thing I was careful to avoid was giving Mom the impression that she might be moving into our home with us.

"I found a gorgeous place for you to live, and it is only fifteen minutes from me," I emphasized.

"Oh! That sounds marvelous," she cooed.

"Well, I'm going to talk it over with John and Tink, and if they are okay with it, I'd like you to move here with us."

"As long as they are okay with me moving," Mom said. Of course, my brothers had already agreed that if Mom were willing, we'd make the move.

Chapter 11

MAKING THE MOVE

Dressed in a purple jacket, black slacks, and her favorite white tennis shoes, Mom looked so happy as she slowly made her way up the Nashville airport concourse. Meanwhile, John and our nephew Marc were transporting the sum total of her belongings to Nashville in John's pickup truck. Lisa and I furnished her apartment with items from our home, and it really looked nice when she arrived. Still, it was emotionally difficult for Mom leaving her Florida family members. Despite her excitement, I could tell that she was a bit afraid too.

To help allay Mom's fears about living alone in a new environment, we hung a large picture of Jesus above the headboard of her bed. In the painting, Jesus has His arms open to the world, as though inviting all to come to the party. We put a slightly mystical, though not inaccurate, twist on the painting.

"Look, Mom. Jesus is here with you," I told her, "and He has

His arms outstretched to remind you that He is going to take good care of you."

"Oh, that's beautiful," she said. "That makes me feel much better."

After moving Mom's belongings into her new apartment, John and I walked outside and talked candidly. "I'm convinced the thing she fears the most is that she's never going to see you guys again," I said. "With most of the family members in Florida, she's thinking, 'I'll never get back to Orlando, and they won't come here to see me. I'll probably die before I see them again.'"

John agreed, and we talked further about the need for our family members to visit Mom as often as possible, to call or write, and to remain part of her life. John's eyes welled with tears as he said good-bye to Mom and he and Marc pointed the truck back toward Orlando.

The transition wasn't easy, but with the help of the staff at the Manor, Mom soon made friends. Before long she joined residents for breakfast and morning exercises. She also discovered the house piano. The small baby grand featured a volume control on the side of the keyboard and accommodated prerecorded CDs, or it could be played as an acoustic piano.

When Mom began playing the instrument, she was not familiar with the volume controls. The piano blared and some of the residents complained even louder. Many of them enjoyed Mom's piano playing, however, especially since she knew so many old hymns. They called out their favorites, and Mom played them all without written music. The "old-timers" were amazed, and Mom felt accepted and right at home.

As part of the process of relocating, we had to find all new doctors for Mom. She had arrived carrying a sack filled with medications that she had been taking while living in Florida, many of which we had no idea when or why the medicine had been prescribed. One of the first things we decided to do was to get Mom a checkup to determine if all those drugs were necessary. We discovered about half of her medications dated back to when she had been living in Pennsylvania. Apparently it is rare for a doctor to remove a medication from a patient. Once prescribed, the medication remains on the records and insurance documentation forever. Or at least it seems that way, because no physician ever took Mom off any medication. Instead, the doctors simply upped the dosages or added new pills to her already confusing and often contradictory regimen. For example, when Mom arrived in Tennessee, she was taking a "water pill," a pill that helped her to go to the bathroom; at the same time, she was taking another pill that impeded urination. Can you imagine that? *Go! No, stop! Go; no, don't.* No wonder her body was rebelling!

We arranged for Mom to be examined regularly by a geriatric physician, Dr. Stephen D'Amico. Although we didn't know it when we made the appointment, Dr. D'Amico is one of the premier doctors in his field. It took only one appointment for him to figure out that Mom was suffering from dementia. I wasn't along for Mom's first meeting with the doctor, but in subsequent appointments, I accompanied my mom and Lisa. Initially, I was put off by Dr. D'Amico's style. The doctor came in and looked over Mom's bloodwork chart and the results of other tests that had been done since her previous appointment. He talked briefly with my mom, asking a few personal questions and some simple questions about current events, with us in the room. Then, with Mom sitting a mere three feet away, he turned to Lisa and me and said bluntly, "I'm not going to pull any punches with you. This is not going to get better."

I was somewhere between offended and horrified that he was speaking so frankly in front of my mother. More importantly, I totally disagreed with him. After all, we were Christians. Whatever ailments Mom suffered were subject to the power of God. We believed in God's ability to heal a body, mind, and spirit. Although I didn't say it at the time, I thought, *Don't tell me my mom is not going to get better. I don't believe that, and I am not going to accept your negative assumptions.*

Back home Lisa reminded me what the doctor had said. "Ken, he may be right."

"Nah," I said with a wave of my hand. "My mom has always been a bit forgetful. And asking her questions like, 'What is the president's name?' just doesn't compute. I doubt she's paid much attention to a president since Nixon. If the doctor had asked her a question from the Bible, Mom could have wowed him."

"Maybe so, but you need to consider the possibility that the doctor sees something in your mom that we don't."

In retrospect, it's easy to recognize that I was in denial, but when you are in the midst of it, especially in the beginning stages of your parent becoming your child, denial is the last thing on your mind. I didn't want to admit that something was wrong with my mom.

She's always done quirky, zany things, I told myself. *She's old— that's all—other than that she's just fine.* Besides, God had raised her up from her sickbed many times. I'd been with Mom when she was too sick to stand up, but still she got out of bed, went on stage, and performed in a concert. Whatever this thing was, God was greater, and Mom could beat it. I refused to accept the idea that perhaps something had happened to her that had irreparably damaged her mind, that she was on an inexorable downhill slide and nothing was going to stop it—not even God.

Chapter 12

THE SPIRITUAL MATTERS

Mom enjoyed living at the Manor, but as she had done in Florida, she soon began accusing people of stealing her stuff—her underwear, her television remote control (which was usually under the bed), her blue jeans. Again, we were unaware that these accusations stemmed from dementia, and simply tried to reassure Mom that she was in a safe environment. Meeting fellow Christians at the Manor seemed to help assuage Mom's concerns.

One friend Mom came to especially love was Jolene Gardner, a widowed preacher's wife. The two of them struck up an instant friendship. Jolene was in her seventies, and also had dementia, but was still somewhat cogent, although she did have a habit of repeating herself. One day, when Lisa and I picked up Mom for church, she got in the car and lamented, "Jolene's losing it. She tells me the same story over and over!" Which of course was exactly what my mom did to us. Every Sunday, she told us about the Methodist church van that transported seniors from the Manor to church.

"That's nice that the Methodist church does that," I played along.

"Yes, there are quite a few Methodists here," she said. I wasn't sure if Mom thought that was a good thing or a bad thing, but she told me about it every week.

Besides attending weekly Bible studies and special worship services at the Manor, Mom attended church services regularly along with us. I taught Sunday school at our church, and Mom proudly sat right up front, saying "Amen" to almost everything I said. People in the class loved my mom, and treated her like a queen, and Mom loved that.

"We really enjoy Ken's teaching," someone might say to her.

"That's just the way I taught him," she'd say with a twinkle in her eye.

"Miss Minnie," as the people in class called her, was a term of respectful familiarity. Sometimes she'd make off-the-wall comments and our fellow parishioners would give me knowing looks. I'd just smile and raise my eyebrows, as if to say, "Sorry; please excuse my mom's blunt statements," but despite her sometimes embarrassing comments, I was always glad to have her with me. Mom was thrilled to be in our class, and the honor showered on her by class members gave her a sense of significance.

Although Mom's short-term memory was impaired, she possessed a deep reservoir of Scripture and a vibrant relationship with Christ, so I shouldn't have been surprised that there remained a residue within her that the Holy Spirit could draw out and use. One night, at the close of the church service, the pastor asked us to join together with the people closest to us and pray for each other. Marie, a member of the church staff, was sitting next to my mom and me. I introduced Marie to Mom and asked Mom to pray for her; Mom didn't know anything about Marie, but she prayed a marvelous prayer—guided, I believe, by the Holy Spirit—and it made a profound impact on Marie.

"Can I have lunch with Minnie someday?" Marie asked with tears in her eyes.

"Sure thing," I replied, guessing that Mom would probably not even remember Marie's name by the time we left the building.

On Wednesday and Sunday nights, church sometimes ran long or we stopped to get something to eat after the service. On those occasions we kept Mom out after the main doors at the Manor were locked. Since the residents had their own apartments in an independent living environment, the Manor did not dictate when they should come and go, but for security purposes, the automatic sliding doors at the front entryway were locked at 9:00 p.m. After that, residents were required to use their keys to enter a back or side door. Mom lived on the third floor, far from the elevators. If we entered a side door, she had to walk the entire length of the first floor to reach an elevator, then traverse the full distance of the third floor. To save steps, we often trudged up three levels of stairs to get directly to her hallway.

Going up the back stairwell was no easy matter. Mom grunted and grumbled with each step. Lisa, Alyssa, John, or whoever happened to be with us held on to one of Mom's hands and gently pulled her up the stairwell. Mom held on to a handrail, and I stood behind her, my hands on her waist, my shoulder under her behind, to give her a little more "umph," and sometimes helping her to lift her foot high enough to make the next step. It was slow, tedious work. Every once in a while, she would tilt backward precariously, and I feared she might fall. But she never did. She struggled inch by inch with each step, refusing to give up. Lisa and I cheered her on.

"One more step, Grandma Minnie," Lisa prodded.

"You can do it, Mom," I added.

By the time we ascended the three flights of stairs, we were exhausted. Mom waddled down the remaining hallway to her apartment, with Lisa holding one arm and me holding the other. I had noticed that she was having difficulty remembering which apartment was hers, so as we walked, I pointed out various paintings on the wall, a set of chairs in the hallway or a flower display, just to give her some Hansel-and-Gretel-style landmarks on the journey from the stairwell to her apartment. Her memory was slipping fast, but silly me, I didn't think it was a serious problem. I simply needed to help her more, I thought.

Every time we took Mom home, Lisa checked over Mom's pills, replenishing and checking to make sure she had taken the medications we had loaded in her pillbox the last time. Then Lisa helped her get ready for bed while I searched for the consistently lost TV remote control. She often hid it (probably so no one would steal it), and then she couldn't remember where she had stashed it. So while Lisa helped Mom into her nightclothes, I crawled around on the floor, looking under her bed, her dresser, just about anywhere there was some open space trying to locate the remote. Once I found it, I'd reprogram it, since inevitably Mom had pressed a button eliminating her television's cable capacity, limiting her viewing to one or two local stations.

Before we left, I always selected a Christian station for Mom to watch until she fell asleep. We also provided Mom some soothing Christian music, and placed a CD player and radio on her bed stand. I felt it was important to keep her mind filled with good, God-honoring messages.

Every night, before saying good-bye, we huddled in a sort of group hug, and we prayed together. Usually Lisa or I prayed for Mom to have a peaceful, safe night. Then after our prayers were completed, Mom would break into prayer, praying for us, making sure to include every need we had, plus praying for all the kids, as well as all the missionaries in Africa. I wasn't sure whether Mom enjoyed praying for us or simply was extending her prayer so we would stay longer. But they were precious prayers, each one.

It was always tough to leave Mom, but I knew she was in a good place. She still had her independence at the Manor, as well as a community of senior adult friends, and she was happy being able to spend so much time with us. In many ways, it was the ideal situation.

A major music event at our church was the annual worship conference. Pastors, musicians, and worship leaders from around the nation and from several foreign countries gathered for four days of nonstop singing, seminars, and spiritual encouragement. A number of well-known music artists shared the evening concerts, creating a smorgasbord of great gospel music for the audiences.

Mom loved the music of the Christ Church Choir, founded and directed by Landy Gardner (Jolene's son) and featuring his wife, Joy, seen often on Bill and Gloria Gaither's *Homecoming* television programs. Since Mom moved to Nashville in mid-June, we had pumped up her enthusiasm for the conference, and she was excited to attend.

Each evening, as the music moved from upbeat, joyful jubilation to a slower, more deliberate worshipful mood, I watched Mom out of the corner of my eye. Slowly, almost imperceptibly at first, she tilted her head back, closed her eyes, and raised her hands above her head as expressions of praise and adoration of the Lord. She often did something similar during our Sunday services. As I observed my mom worshipping God so unabashedly, I thought, *It's worth moving her here just to see that.*

Chapter 13

. . . .

ACCEPTING REALITY

I reluctantly came to accept Dr. D'Amico's diagnosis, so I read some of the materials he suggested and studied more about Alzheimer's and dementia. For the first time I realized that Mom wasn't merely getting old; she was afflicted with a disease, an illness from which she would most likely never recover while here on earth. I now understood that so many of the things she said and did were not personality quirks, as I had previously thought, but were direct results of the dementia. Indeed, I was amazed that so many of the characteristics Mom displayed were similar to other Alzheimer's patients. Although this new awareness deeply saddened me, it also helped me to understand what we were dealing with and enabled me to better cope with the changes.

Perhaps one of the most significant insights I received from my reading on the subject was that most Alzheimer's and dementia victims die within five to fifteen years of being diagnosed. Mom was in her mid-eighties; time was not on our side.

I began keeping notes on Mom's progress—or regress, depending on one's perspective. I didn't really know what to expect, other than recognizing more of the signs of dementia that I had studied, so I didn't write down everything she did and said. But I wanted to create a loose record, a journal of sorts, marking dates and tracking Mom's demise, keeping memories of the real Minnie Abraham alive while trying to understand and care for this new childlike Minnie. My journal entries looked like this:

September 26, 2008—

She now realizes that she is losing her memory; she knows she can't remember what day it is, quite literally, and it bothers her immensely. But there's nothing I can do about it. The nurse who is trying to help with her memory has all but given up; she's tried all her tricks and Mom still can't remember which pills to take or when, and the danger of taking too much Coumadin, a strong blood thinner, is quite real. She needs the Coumadin to prevent blood clots in her heart or brain and thus running the risk of a more severe stroke, which could be incapacitating. Her heart is enlarged and has an irregular heartbeat but it is a "consistent irregularity," as the doctor describes it, supposedly the "best" sort of atrial fibrillation that an elderly person could have.

I'd like to see her get off all of that medication and then see what happens. But the threat of an incapacitating stroke scares me. Do I have faith that the Lord could take care of her, that He could even heal her? Yes, I do . . . I think. But do I want to risk it right now? I'm not so sure about that.

"What day is tomorrow?" Mom asked me on the phone.

"Tomorrow is Tuesday, Mom," I told her.

"Isn't tomorrow Saturday?"

"No, Mom; tomorrow is Tuesday."

"Okay, I'll see you on Saturday." 'Round and 'round we went. It was the dementia version of "Who's on First?"

Exacerbated by her memory matters, handling Mom's medication became a major control issue for us. She continually failed to take her prescribed medication or took incorrect dosages, so we confiscated all her meds and doled them out in small daily allotments. Not surprisingly, Mom didn't appreciate that at all.

Mom had always gone to the doctor and pharmacy on her own. She took her own medicines whenever they were prescribed. Now, however, she seemed unable to keep her pills straight, so from the time Mom moved to Tennessee, Lisa and I became actively involved in monitoring her medications. She was taking eight pills each day when she arrived, and under Dr. D'Amico's watchful eye, we were able to pare that number in half. Still, she had four important medications to take daily, and it was a constant battle to get her to take the right pills in the correct number on the appropriate day of the week.

At first, we naively placed the full bottles of pills in Mom's kitchen cupboard. After all, she'd always handled her own medications in the past. We soon learned, however, an important lesson for all caregivers of Alzheimer's and dementia patients: It is not enough to monitor medication. We had to take control of what pills Mom put in her mouth every day. Otherwise she'd get the wrong ones, or too many, or not enough.

We purchased plastic pillboxes, with seven separate compartments with individual caps to help separate her daily pills. Mom still mixed them together. We put up a calendar on her door, so she could mark off which pills she took each day. She did fairly well with that at first, until we realized that just because she marked off the day did not necessarily mean that she had taken the pills. It was a constant battle as we tried to make sure she took the appropriate medications. The task was more difficult because some pills were to be taken in the morning, and others at night. When we were with her, one of our first questions was always, "Mom, have you taken your pills?"

"Of course I have," she'd say.

But when we checked the pillboxes, oftentimes the pills were still there. Before leaving Mom each day, Lisa or I checked her pills and made her take them in front of us. That let us know that she had taken the appropriate pills for the moment, but we had little ability to control what she'd take once we were out of the room. We saw an ad in a magazine featuring a gizmo that used a timer to release pills at the appropriate time and in the right dosages. We came close to trying it, but never did.

We also discovered that it was no longer wise to let Mom select her own clothing. She never dressed immodestly; thankfully, wearing conservative apparel remained ingrained in her psyche. But she tended to dress tacky, and that set her apart from the majority of the women at the Manor, many of whom came from wealthy, sophisticated backgrounds, and continued their habits of dressing well, wearing expensive looking jewelry, and applying appropriate makeup and perfume every day. Mom, however, was content to dress in whatever she pulled out of her closets, often resulting in a Miss Rummage Sale look, layering herself with various styles and colors of clothes that didn't match.

To make dressing easier, Lisa sorted all of Mom's outfits and dresses, hanging slacks and blouses together in attractive combinations in her closets. Nevertheless, Mom continually mixed and matched items that didn't look good together. So Lisa would do it all over again, matching Mom's outfits into beautiful sets. A few days later, her closets looked like a tornado had swept through.

"Gram! Just wear the clothes that we've matched for you," Lisa implored. "You'll look adorable."

"I do wear the clothes you hang up for me."

"No, you don't. You put plaids together with stripes, and orange together with purple, and things get all mixed up. Ken wants you to look good. We've bought you some beautiful clothes, so just wear them the way they are matched together."

One Sunday morning, when we picked up Mom for church, she had on an outrageous combination of clothes. The night before, Lisa and Alyssa and I had picked out a lovely red dress and jacket for her to wear, but in the light of Sunday morning, Mom had decided that the dress was too big because it came down too far below her knees. She had replaced it with a variety of old favorites.

"Gram, the look of that red dress is in style." Lisa tried to encourage her to change her outfit.

"Oh, I don't care about style."

"No, but we do."

And so it went, week after week. One Sunday morning Mom came down from her apartment ready to go to church wearing slacks and her white tennis shoes. While that look was fine during the week, we always encouraged our girls to wear dresses to church on Sunday morning. Despite her protests, we made Mom go back upstairs and change. Alyssa accompanied her to help.

"I'm sick of this," she groused to Alyssa, as she put on a dress. "I have too many bosses!"

Hannah Crockett and Sarah Blair, two delightful Christian young women—both single at the time—had taken Mom out on the town when she first moved to Nashville. Mom loved Sarah and Hannah. When Hannah got engaged, she graciously included an invitation for Mom to attend her wedding shower. At the shower, Mom came in to the party and greeted Hannah, "Well, have you found a man yet?"

"Yes, Grandma Minnie," Hannah replied. "This is my wedding shower. I have a great fiancé named Clay Tate."

"Well, that's nice; but have you found a fella yet?"

Now that Mom was living in close proximity to us, Lisa took her to her doctors' appointments, which was almost like a full-time job in itself. Mom thanked her sincerely, but she could also be quite obstreperous with Lisa, sometimes saying hurtful things. She had done something similar with my sisters-in-law, Brenda and Sandie, when she lived in Florida, but at that time, they didn't understand that Mom was speaking out of the disease, not necessarily her right mind or heart. Consequently, they grew tired of her cantankerousness, and eventually threw up protective barriers around their own emotions.

Lisa, however, had gone to my mom's doctors' appointments with her, and had tracked right along with each physician's assessments of Mom's dementia. It wasn't any easier for her to take the brunt of Mom's verbal blows, but she at least had the luxury of understanding that the real Minnie had long since disappeared. We were now hearing an octogenarian parent with whom we often had to deal as a child—a child we could not discipline and whose mind was difficult if not impossible to change.

Studying more about Alzheimer's and dementia, I found that stubbornness, unwarranted complaints, petulance, unrealistic demands, and inordinate or inappropriate suspicions went with the territory. We noticed all of those characteristics showing up more frequently in Mom's behavior.

When it came to stubbornness, Mom had that trait down, especially regarding her habits of cleanliness. Cleanliness is next to godliness, she had taught us as kids. Mom had never been fastidious about her housekeeping or her personal appearance, yet she had always been clean. Now, however, like many people afflicted with dementia, she shied away from the bathtub. Her shower and tub unit at the Manor was constructed with a low entry, several assistance bars, and a built-in seat. But for some reason, Mom preferred a "sponge bath," washing in front of her sink, outside the tub. Eventually, we figured out that she was not even getting inside the sit-down shower in her apartment. Whether it was fear of falling or that she simply could not remember how to operate the showerhead and water faucets, I wasn't certain.

Oddly enough, whenever she had visited with us prior to the onset of dementia, Mom bathed or showered every day. She had always preferred baths, but was not opposed to taking a shower. Until the dementia set in. Now she seemed reticent to even get in the shower at her apartment, and she particularly did not want to wash her hair.

Although Mom had beautiful, wavy hair—a trait about which she beamed—Mom stopped washing her hair, especially with shampoo. The first shampoo we bought her had a coconut scent that Mom disliked. That's strange, I thought; she has always loved coconut because it reminded her of the Hawaiian vacations we enjoyed. We purchased a different brand of shampoo, and she didn't like that one either. Finally I found an empty Redken shampoo bottle and filled it with a much less expensive brand. Mom knew that I had always used Redken hair-care products when I lived at home, and she developed an affinity for the same brand.

"Oh, yes, that's perfect," she said when we gave her the fake Redken.

"Did you wash your hair today?" I asked almost every day we visited.

"Of course I did," Mom replied.

"Did you use shampoo?"

"Ken!" she huffed. "Yes, I used shampoo."

I opened the Redken bottle and looked inside. It was full to the brim. Either Mom didn't use the shampoo and thought she had, or she wasn't using anything at all. We repeatedly encouraged her to take a shower every day and to use shampoo on her hair since it looked as though she was not washing it sufficiently.

"I do take a shower every morning," she staunchly stated. "And I wash my hair too."

"But Gram," Lisa gently chided, "the shampoo that we brought to you several weeks ago is still full."

"Well, I don't use as much as you people do."

"No, it looks as though you haven't used any at all."

And so it went.

Lisa tried a different approach. She bought a new outfit for Mom, and told her that I really wanted her to wash her hair before putting it on. "Ken would have come over to help you himself, but he thought that you might be embarrassed," Lisa told her.

"Yes, he'd be right," Mom responded.

After Lisa helped her take a shower and wash her hair, Mom was sitting on the commode, drying her feet. She looked up and said, "Lisa, don't ever get old. I used to hear old people complaining about how they couldn't do this or that, and I'd think, 'What's your problem? Get over it.' But now I understand."

Chapter 14
. . . .

UNWARRANTED
ACCUSATIONS AND
INCESSANT PHONE
CALLS

"They're stealing from me again," Mom said on her phone message to me. "They took the card that Tink sent to me for Christmas. And they stole my flicker (the television remote control). Something is going to have to be done, Ken. They're robbing me blind here!"

Mom's accusations about someone stealing from her often centered around Beverly, one of the housekeepers at the Manor. Ordinarily I ignored Mom's aspersions, but when other people at the Manor confirmed that items in their apartments were missing, I wondered whether there was some credence in Mom's complaints.

I mentioned the matter to the activities director, and she assured me that many of the residents were just as bad as my mom when it came to being suspicious or making false accusations.

Because of Mom's recent propensity to get confused, it was always a fine line trying to determine who was right or wrong in dealing with questions regarding the maids or maintenance people at the Manor. I wanted to give the help staff the benefit of the doubt, recognizing that Mom might have been seeing things through dim glasses; yet on the other hand, she was still my mom, and I didn't want people taking advantage of her or mistreating her in any way. Nor did I automatically assume that simply because Mom had dementia she was confused about the facts. I was all too aware of situations in which elderly folks had been ripped off by "caregivers." On the other hand, with her memory slipping, Mom didn't always get things exactly right.

One day when Lisa went to the Manor, Mom was complaining to Beverly that she had not cleaned her apartment as often as required. While Beverly worked in her room, Mom castigated her for not giving her clean towels.

"Now, Minnie, that's not so," Beverly said amiably. "I cleaned your apartment yesterday. And I changed your towels too."

"You did?"

"Yes, ma'am, I did. Don't you remember? I'm beginning to get worried about you. You're forgetting things."

"Well, I'm beginning to get worried about you too," Mom answered without missing a beat. "You have a blue light blinking in your ear!"

"What?"

"Right there!" Mom pointed at Beverly's ear.

Beverly reached up and realized what Mom was seeing. "Oh, Minnie, that's the earpiece for my cell phone!" she said. "Here, let me put it on you, and I'll show you." Beverly attached the cell phone speaker over Mom's ear, then had her sister talk to Mom on the headset.

"Well, I'm glad it is a phone," Mom said. "Because I was really worried about you for a while!"

Incessant phone calls revealed further symptoms of Mom's dementia. I asked her dozens of times to call on my home line, since my cell phone plan had a limited number of minutes. But fifteen to twenty times a day, she'd call on my cell. She rarely remembered calling previously.

Moreover, after an initial hefty long distance bill, we changed Mom's phone service so she no longer had long distance, and could only call my brothers by using a prepaid calling card—which she promptly lost. No problem. She remembered how to dial zero, which put her in contact with an operator who unwittingly connected her to my brothers. When her next phone bill noted an enormous amount due for "operator-assisted calls," I contacted the phone company and naively threatened to sue them for taking advantage of a senior citizen with dementia. The phone company supposedly inserted a notation that operator-assisted calls were not permissible from Mom's phone.

That helped, but not much. I later realized that, although Mom had easily used a prepaid phone card when she was well, it was too much for her now that she had trouble remembering the numbers to dial, even though they were listed on the back of the card. The instructions were too detailed, and there were too many steps for her to process. She often called me and asked, "Do you have your brother John's phone number? I've been trying to call him all night and my calls won't go through."

"Have you been using your phone cards?"

After a pause, she'd say, "No . . ."

"Your call won't go through, Mom, unless you dial the toll-free number on the phone card and then follow the instructions."

"Well, okay, I'll just try to get him tomorrow."

I knew what that meant. She didn't want to bother with the phone card. Her inability to use the card revealed a new element about dementia that we were now encountering—namely, experts suggest that a person with dementia can handle only one piece of information at a time. In the past, I could tell my mom, "Just dial the 800 number and when the operator comes on, punch in the pin number, and then you can dial your number." Now Mom couldn't recall that many instructions. "Dial the 800 number," was about as far as she could get. When I attempted to help her use the phone cards to call John or Tink, she quickly grew frustrated.

"It's okay," she said, "I'll call them later."

Of course she never did, unless it was on my brothers' toll-free work numbers that had been stuck in her mind for years. My brothers repeatedly reminded Mom not to call them on those lines unless there was an emergency, but everything was an emergency to Mom. In fairness to Mom, she wasn't disrespecting my brothers or their employers. Those toll-free numbers were the only ones she could remember other than mine.

Mom's ability to dial phone numbers diminished rapidly that winter, but she still managed to call me numerous times each day. I answered when I could, but when I was working, often her calls went directly to voice mail.

"Hi, Ken, this is Mom. Please call me. My phone number is . . ." Five months after receiving her new phone number, she still reminded me of it several times a day. "Please call me; I'm confused. I don't know what day it is. I'm ready for church, but nobody else seems to be going. Somebody told me that it is Tuesday, not

Sunday, so no wonder you haven't come to pick me up yet. Please call me back."

"Hi, Ken; this is Mom . . ." she recorded on my voice mail and then paused. She stayed on the line for a few seconds, but when I didn't pick up the phone, she breathed a sigh of exasperation, and said simply, "I love you."

When I heard the message, I buried my face in my hands and closed my eyes in a futile attempt to pretend it wasn't happening, but it was. I could no longer deny the truth. Mom was indeed "losing it," as she put it; she thought that she was losing a bit of her memory when, in fact, she was losing the battle with dementia.

Mom loved Bob Barker, host of the television show *The Price Is Right*. She grieved when Barker retired, but she came to appreciate Drew Carey when he took over as emcee of the show. She often called me close to the time *The Price Is Right* aired in Nashville, so if I didn't have much time to talk, I'd say, "Mom, your show is coming on soon."

"What show?"

"*The Price Is Right*."

"Oh, okay. I'll talk to you later. Bye." And she was gone.

I'd hang up the telephone and thank God for Bob Barker and Drew Carey.

A positive aspect of Mom losing her memory was that we didn't have to worry about offending her; if she got upset about something, she usually would not remember the next day. She was like the fellow who went to the airport to pick up his aging mother-in-law who had dementia. "So good of you to come," he said. "Have a nice flight home."

Chapter 15

. . . .

MEMORY PROBLEMS? WHAT MEMORY PROBLEMS?

In the Manor dining room, Mom often stopped by a large fruit bowl that was refilled throughout the day so residents could snack on fruit rather than sugar-loaded products. Mom snatched bananas, apples, and oranges from the dining room on a regular basis, hoarding them in her refrigerator. The fruit remained in the refrigerator until Lisa or I conducted a routine check and discovered a fridge chock-full of moldy fruit.

Hoarding, we later discovered, is another common trait associated with dementia patients. When Mom wouldn't eat her cache of fruit, we'd haul it out of her apartment to keep it from spoiling any further. But when I'd say, "Mom, please don't take more fruit than you are going to eat," she'd get huffy and say,

"That's why they have it there. Everyone takes extra for snacks later in the day."

"But Mom, that's stealing!"

"It's not stealing. That's why they put the fruit out there, for us to take."

"Okay, Mom. But you don't need to take enough for everyone in town."

Truth is, my mom didn't even like fruit.

Dr. D'Amico, Mom's geriatric doctor, suggested that she visit a neurologist because her memory problems were becoming more severe. At her first appointment the neurologist greeted Mom and Lisa in the waiting room.

"And this is my daughter-in-law, Lisa," Mom introduced Lisa again. They stood up and followed the doctor into his examination room, where Mom asked again, "Did you meet my daughter-in-law, Lisa?" A few more feet into the exam room, they sat down, and Mom turned to the doctor again. "Did you meet my daughter-in-law, Lisa?"

The doctor said yes every time.

Then the first question he posed was, "Minnie, I hear you have been having some problems with your memory. Is that right?"

"Oh, no. I have a great memory," she told the doctor. "I'm not having any problems!"

The doctor never let on that he thought otherwise. He did, however, issue a battery of tests to check Mom's ability to remember facts and handle abstract concepts.

After the exam, Mom told Lisa, "I think everyone should take that memory test. It will help them remember things." Then she paused to reconsider. "I know Ken is smart, but I don't think even he could have done well on that test. It was really hard!"

The doctor had asked her questions such as, "What is the president's name? Who is your US Senator?" Mom didn't know. On the way home (a week before the 2008 presidential election), she asked, "Who *is* the president of the United States?" As for the doctor asking about her senators: "That wasn't fair. I haven't even lived in Tennessee that long."

On the plus side, even though dementia dogged her, Mom retained her sense of humor. After a long day of doctors' visits, Mom returned to the Manor, where one of the female residents asked, "How'd it go, Minnie?"

"Well, I'm not pregnant!" she deadpanned.

Most dementia experts suggest that people who have the disease may be able to recall long-term history, presenting the illusion to loved ones that the mind is still intact and functioning well, but the dementia victim cannot learn new information. Mom, however, broke that mold. During an evening service at our church, the worship team led the congregation in singing "Revelation Song," a recently written number based on Scripture. Mom possessed a vast repertoire of music that she knew from playing the piano in church over the years, but she had not learned that particular song earlier in life. She'd learned it only since she had been in Tennessee. As the congregation sang the new song in a service, Mom sang along and didn't miss a beat. Later in the car, she was singing that same melody.

"I just love that song," she said.

Just goes to show that doctors don't know everything. Her mind, or at least her spirit, was able to learn something new if it was meaningful to her.

Knowing that Mom never cared much for Halloween, with its emphasis on devils and demons, we decided to take her to a local theater presentation of the musical *Oliver!* on Halloween evening. At first she was a little confused about what was going on. Early in the story, Oliver is treated roughly by his adult keepers, who twist his ear and hold him by his hair as he squirms, trying to get away. Sitting right up front, only six rows away from the stage lights, Mom shook her head and said aloud, "I don't think that's right!"

"Shh, Mom!" I quietly tried to explain to her that it was merely a play, a story, and the boy was only pretending to be in pain.

"Oh," Mom said. "That's better."

Fortunately the actors didn't seem to hear, and the show went on.

Despite the dementia, Mom was still quite social. For Megan's college graduation party, Mom stood at the front door and greeted every person. She knew more of our neighbors by name than I did. One night when John was in town for a visit, we got some backstage passes to the Grand Old Opry. During intermission we circulated backstage among country music stars Ricky Skaggs, Wynonna Judd, and our neighbor Lee Greenwood. Thinking that it would be a treat to introduce Mom to Lee, I said, "Mom, that's Lee Greenwood right there. You know? The fellow who sings the song, 'God Bless the U.S.A.'?"

"Oh, I know him," Mom answered.

Sure you do, I thought as I shook my head and said, "Come on, let's say hello." I guided Mom through the maze of people to where Lee and his wife, Kim, were talking with some friends in the greenroom.

"Hi, Kim; hi, Lee. This is my mom, Minnie Abraham. She's just moved to Nashville from Orlando."

"Oh, hi, Minnie," Lee said warmly. Then looking at me, he

said, "Yes, I know Minnie. I see her walking the dog all the time in the neighborhood. We're good friends."

The baffling dichotomy of dementia: she couldn't remember what day it was, but she knew everyone in the neighborhood.

In the early days of her downward slide into dementia, we noticed that Mom couldn't follow a conversation anymore. Nor could she follow a story line of a movie or television show. When the family gathered to watch a program, Mom quickly grew bored. At first I thought she simply wasn't interested or was not enjoying the show. But then I realized that her brain could not process the plot. It was too much information for her. Due to the disease, she could handle stories in short sections, but not much more. She preferred game shows such as *Wheel of Fortune*, and she always recognized Vanna White.

"That Vanna is really something," Mom told me dozens of times, not necessarily complimenting the star letter-turner.

Changing the subject rather than arguing is a key to dealing with someone afflicted with dementia, so I attempted to turn the subject around positively. "Yeah, she's really nice, isn't she?" I offered, as though Vanna and I were best friends.

Mom's tone changed immediately. "Oh, yeah," she said. "I love watching her."

Lisa noticed the difference in my mom's ability to help in the kitchen, which she constantly volunteered to do. But now, more than one task stymied her. We could say, "Gram, please peel these potatoes." But it was useless to say, "Peel the potatoes, then put them in the pan of water, and put it on the stove. When they are cooked, take them off and mash them." Mom couldn't process more than one instruction, and she became agitated when she couldn't remember what she was supposed to do. After we realized her dilemma and discovered that most dementia victims have difficulty with multiple instructions, we were careful to give her only one task at a time. When she completed that, we'd give her something else to do. Mom enjoyed helping, so once we found how she best functioned, it was a blessing for all of us.

Mom joined us for Thanksgiving 2008, so I prepared an abundant plateful of food for her. When Lisa saw the amount of food on Mom's plate, she was surprised. "Wow, Grandma Minnie must really be enjoying the day!"

Mom ate very little of the food that I dished out for her, but that was okay. She enjoyed being at the table and listening to the testimonies of friends and family members who, as we usually did at Thanksgiving, gave reports of recent illustrations of the goodness of God in their lives. Mom smiled often, and interjected more than a few times with, "Hallelujah," "Praise the Lord," and "Thank you, Jesus."

We joked about it, but we all knew that she would not be with us for many more events like this, and even if she was, she wouldn't be able to remember them. I was determined to make her life as joyful as possible during this time of cogency, such as it was.

Joining us later in the living room, Mom sat on the couch with the kids, but she didn't relish being in an environment filled with loud, excited voices as we played games after dinner. We know now that most people afflicted with dementia are disturbed by loud noises or too much excitement, but at the time we simply thought Mom was tired.

Christmas is a dilemma when dealing with a person afflicted with dementia. Loneliness is even more pronounced during the holidays, so we made special efforts to include Mom in as many activities as possible. Of course, she couldn't go shopping; she tired much too quickly. Worse yet, she wanted to buy something for everyone in the family, but her financial resources were quite limited. While we had plenty of gifts for Mom, she felt depressed because she couldn't shop for everyone else.

For her first Christmas in her Tennessee apartment, she had a tiny artificial Christmas tree in the corner of her living room. It saddened me even to look at that pathetic tree. Moreover, the tree reminded me that, one of these days, Mom would be home with Jesus for Christmas. She wouldn't be worried about procuring an evergreen tree or not having enough money to buy presents for everyone. On that day, she would be evergreen, and the many presents that she sent up to heaven in the form of prayers and gifts to the Lord would be generously rewarded. Keeping that perspective helped a bit.

Mom enjoyed the many concerts and programs at our church during the holiday season. But the church campus is a large sprawling complex and Mom tended to get lost easily in the buildings.

After Sunday school Mom inevitably had to go to the restroom. At first we'd wait for Mom in the hallway, but after about fifteen minutes of her just sitting on the commode contemplating the great issues of life, we decided to let her take her time.

"Mom, how are you doing in there?" I'd call from outside the restroom door. "Do you need any help?" Dealing with a dementia patient causes one to lose all sense of pride and inhibitions.

"No, no; I'm fine."

"Okay, meet us in the sanctuary, Mom," I'd say. "You know where we sit." And she did know where we sat—we'd sat in the same general area of the church for years, but she just couldn't remember which section of the church. So week after week, sometimes as much as thirty to forty minutes after the service had begun, she'd waddle into the sanctuary, make her way down to the front of the church and then back up to where we were seated in the side balcony. People in our church probably thought, "Those terribly mean Abrahams, letting their mother roam around this huge church like that! How inconsiderate!"

Sometimes she'd meet someone in the restroom and strike up a conversation. Before long she'd be praying for the woman right there in a stall or at the sink. After a while, the woman would come out of the restroom, refreshed and revived, both physically and spiritually. We often teased that Mom had a powerfully moving "restroom ministry."

One Sunday Mom slept through the entire sermon, which was not easy to do since our minister was an energetic and enthusiastic speaker. And Mom really enjoyed his sermons when she heard them. That particular morning, throughout the service I'd glance over at her just to make sure she was okay. She'd nod forward every so often, but other than that was sleeping peacefully, despite the preacher's emphatic and loud presentation.

At the conclusion of the message, we stood to sing a closing congregational song. Mom stood too. She looked over at me, and as dead serious as could be, said, "That was a great sermon, wasn't it?"

I didn't know whether to burst into tears or burst out laughing.

A few weeks before one of her doctors' appointments, Mom said she wasn't feeling well and didn't want to go to church on Sunday morning. Nor did she want to go to Wednesday night Bible study, which was unusual for her. That should have been a sign to us, but unfortunately, since we still didn't realize how dementia slowly takes over a person's brain and personality, we didn't pick up on the change in Mom's demeanor.

At the next appointment, however, the doctor asked Lisa if we could discern any difference in Mom's actions since he had prescribed a new medicine that was supposed to help her memory. (None of the medicine ever did help her memory, incidentally.)

"No, we can't really tell any difference," Lisa told the doctor. "But, not long ago, Minnie didn't want to go to church with us on Sunday or Wednesday, and that's just not like her."

The doctor looked at my mom and she nodded her head. "That's just not like me," she told him. "Not like me at all!"

But of course it was.

Chapter 16

THE SENILE LEADING
THE SENILE

In March 2009, Lisa and I went to Cancun with our children for spring break. We let Mom keep Pumpkin, our docile fifteen-year-old poodle who had just been to the vet the week before and officially pronounced senile. He was almost blind and deaf, but he was still our lovable, huggable poodle and we enjoyed having him as part of our family. We could have had someone house-sit Pumpkin, but we thought we might give Mom the opportunity to keep him since she loved Pumpkin and enjoyed walking him around the neighborhood when she was at our house.

We took Pumpkin to Mom the night before our trip and even went through a "dry run" regarding how Mom could take him outside. We gave her specific instructions that to avoid accidents, she should keep Pumpkin diapered while inside, and we emphasized that any time she went out of the apartment without him, she should put him in his kennel, so he wouldn't scratch her door.

Mom agreed, and it seemed that she understood everything we said. "We'll be fine," she said, giving Pumpkin a hug. "Don't you worry about a thing."

When we returned we discovered that Mom had not kept Pumpkin diapered, nor had she put him in the kennel when she had gone out of her apartment. The results? Yep, accidents on the carpet, and a door that looked like a wild animal was scratching at it, trying to get out. Mom complained of a kink in her neck that had developed, she claimed, after walking the dog all week, and taking him up and down the back steps at the Manor, but she said, "Everybody loves him here!" We translated that to mean that Mom had enjoyed showing off Pumpkin.

Mom loved Pumpkin.
They entered senility together.

When I greeted one of Mom's friends at the Manor, she asked me, "Has your mom gotten rid of that dog yet?" Apparently Mom's comments to others hadn't been as positive as she had been to us. It appeared that Mom loved playing the victim almost as much as the star. I could easily imagine her telling her friends, "Yes, they left this dog with me to care for, and I'm ready to give him back!"

I returned to my office and discovered that while we were gone—a mere Monday through Saturday trip—Mom had called my phone seventy-seven times, leaving messages, thinking that we were home, often asking, "What are you working on today?" or other questions indicating her assumption that I was in my office working near the phone rather than relaxing on the beach in Cancun. As much as we had told her that we would be gone all week, she thought we were going away for an evening, or perhaps not at all.

Over the Easter weekend, the Nashville area was severely struck by tornadoes, resulting in millions of dollars worth of property damaged. A devastating tornado hit in Murfreesboro, a mere thirty minutes from our home. During the storms, Mom was watching the tornado warnings on television and calling us frantically with the latest updates. It was a serious weather alert, but I cracked up when she told me how worried she was about my younger brother getting home from work safely. My brother was in Florida, nearly seven hundred and fifty miles away.

"He'll be fine, Mom. Just pray for him," I said.

"Okay, I will." And I have no doubt that she hung up the phone and spent the next half hour or more praying for my brother. I don't know what God does with those prayers, but maybe my brother needed them for some other reason.

I often felt as though we were living in the Bill Murray movie *Groundhog Day* as we went through almost the exact same phone conversations day after day.

"I'm going down to dinner," Mom would say. "I just wanted you to know in case you called me."

"Okay, Mom; have a good dinner. I'll talk to you later on."

Three minutes later, my phone rang again. "Hi, Ken, I'm going down to dinner," Mom said. "I wanted you to know in case you were trying to call me."

"Okay, Mom; enjoy your dinner," I repeated, never letting on that we had engaged in this same conversation a few minutes previously. Occasionally, when she'd called several times in a row, I'd remind her, "Mom, you already called and told me that."

"Oh, I'm really losing it," she'd say. "I'm sorry to have bothered you."

One day Mom called and was convinced that she had won the Publishers Clearing House Sweepstakes. Knowing the sweepstakes' lead line is "You may have already won!" I wasn't too worried about her missing out on her money. I was much more concerned about her signing up for four-hundred dollars' worth of magazines she'd never read.

"Mom, don't sign anything till I get there. Just put the notice in your drawer; don't let any of your friends send it in for you; just hang on to it till I come over."

Sure enough, the moment I opened her door, Mom began excitedly telling me how she had won five-thousand dollars.

"No, Mom, I'm sorry," I attempted to tell her, "You didn't win anything. They are just trying to get you to buy more magazines."

"Ken," she said in a huff, "I know when I have won something or when I haven't. And it says right here," she spoke louder as she waved something that looked like a yellow computer printout, "that I am a winner."

"You are a winner, alright, Mom, but you haven't won any money lately," I said with a laugh.

Because she was so prone to rip-offs, we rerouted Mom's mail to our house, and we felt compelled to take Mom's checkbook away from her for her own good so she wouldn't purchase everything she saw on television infomercials. She was especially susceptible to television preachers who offered books, trinkets, or other gifts in return for a financial donation, or something free to procure names for their mailing lists.

"Those preachers wouldn't lie on television," she said, when I tried to explain.

Mom received mailings from nearly every preacher whose programs aired on our local stations and many that broadcasted on network television. No doubt the Lord blessed her for giving, but I wondered about the integrity and accountability of ministries appealing to elderly viewers and hitting all the emotional buttons that might evoke donations from people who may no longer have the mental wherewithal to make such decisions.

When John visited in May, we took Mom golfing with us. She couldn't play the game, but I allowed her to drive the golf cart. She loved that, since driving the cart was a substitute for the fact that we would not allow her to drive a car any longer.

We played with Bob Kernodle, a member of our Sunday school class who was in his mid-seventies yet still spry, and Mike Briggs, who had known Mom for years. Neither Bob or Mike minded Mom driving me in another cart.

Mom nearly ran over Mike as we pulled the carts up to the second tee when she hit the gas pedal instead of the brake. As usual, we laughed it off, and Mike good-naturedly chided my mom, "Hey, Minnie, are you trying to improve my prayer life?" It never occurred to us that her brain might no longer be able to differentiate between the pedals, much less send signals to her feet to manipulate them.

Later in the day Mom leaned over in the golf cart, and quietly said to me, "Ken, I have to pee."

"Oh, no, Mom. Not now. We're in the middle of the golf course. Can't you hold it? We'll be done soon, and I'll take you into the clubhouse and you can use the restroom in there."

"No, I need to go. I have to go now or I'm going to pee in my pants."

"Okay, Mom," I said with a sigh. "There are some other players close behind us, so let me tee off, and I'll drive you over to the restroom by hole number four."

"Oh, don't worry. I can find it," she assured me.

"Okay, just stay on the cart path going back the way we came, and you will run right into the restroom."

"No problem," she called as she tramped the pedal and the golf cart lurched forward. "Don't worry. I'll be fine."

I teed up my ball and, still thinking about Mom driving back to the restroom, promptly chunked the shot right into the marshy high weeds, never to be seen again.

I looked over my shoulder, trying to spot Mom on the cart path somewhere, but she was nowhere to be seen. "Uh-oh," I said aloud. "Where'd she go?"

"Disco will come back before you find that ball," Bob quipped.

"I'm not worried about the ball," I said, peering up the fairway. "I'm looking for my mom. Where did she go?"

Just then we saw a golf cart zoom over the knoll, zipping toward another fairway, right into the line of fire for anyone teeing off from that direction. The cart careened around several turns on the cart path and finally broke through a patch of trees, back onto our fairway, Mom grasping the steering wheel for dear life. She veered toward us, sending the golfers scrambling in various directions. Seconds before she was on target to slam into another golf cart on the path, her foot found the brake (although it may have been riding on the brake the whole time, but her brain simply forgot why), and she screeched to a stop right in front of us. Mom's face glistened with perspiration, and her expression was one of sheer terror. "Where have you guys been?" she said. "I couldn't find you anywhere!"

"We've been right here, Mom. The bathroom is right over there," I said, pointing toward the cement block building between the trees, less than fifty yards away. "Where did you go?"

"I don't know," she replied sadly. "I thought I was on the right road."

We still didn't understand that dementia caused Mom to become so easily disoriented. She was lost, but we were the ones who didn't have a clue.

Chapter 17

MIXED BLESSINGS

I n May, Mom attended Alyssa's high school graduation ceremonies, which began with a Sunday morning church service, in which graduates were honored, then the actual graduation ceremony, followed by an exquisite dinner with family and friends. At the close of the evening, as we were saying good-bye, Mom looked at Alyssa and said, "It was a lovely party. Happy Birthday, honey."

Alyssa and I looked at each other and shrugged. (Her birthday is in November.) We both smiled. For all her lapses in memory, Mom was still "Grandma Minnie," and we appreciated having her with us for this special celebration.

May 25, 2009—

Today we're moving Mom into a smaller room at the Manor. She's already moved from a house to a condo to a two-bedroom apartment . . . now she is moving to a studio apartment with just

enough room for a bed, a couch, and maybe a table and some chairs.
A rather depressing juncture, but because of a rate increase at the
Manor, we can no longer afford to keep Mom in the larger apart-
ment. The studio still provides safety and security, but with much
less space. We recently learned that clutter causes overstimulation
for dementia victims, so perhaps having less space will be a mixed
blessing for Mom. The change will be hard for her at first, and I'm
sure she will go to the wrong apartment numerous times following
the move, trying to get her keys to work in the door . . . but it is for
the best. At least she can continue living there . . . with other senior
citizens who do not require assisted living.

After we had spent a day and a half moving Mom from one apartment
to the other and redecorating her walls in exactly the same manner as
they had been in the previous apartment, complete with the picture
of Jesus over her bed, she called me repeatedly, inviting me to come
see her new place. "When are you going to come visit?" she asked.
"I'm in a new apartment, right down the hall. It's little, but it is nice."

"Yes, I know, Mom. Lisa and the girls and I helped you move,
remember?"

"Oh, yes. I remember now," she sighed. "My brain isn't any good
for anything anymore."

"No problem, Mom." I quickly changed the subject.

When Lisa stopped by to check on Mom, she was surprised to
see that her nameplate was removed from the door.

"I know I replaced that nameplate the last time I was here," Lisa
said. "Grandma Minnie, where's your new nameplate on your front
door?" she asked. "I just put a new one on there the other day."

"I took it off," Mom replied bluntly.

"Why?"

"I don't want them to find me," Mom said quietly.

"Who? Your friends?"

"No, my friends know where to find me. I mean the others." The way Mom said "the others," it sounded as if she'd seen too many installments of the television series *Lost*. (Of course Mom had never seen that show.)

"Well, I've replaced your nameplate again," Lisa said. "Do you want me to take it out?"

"No," Mom said with a sigh, "they'll find me anyway."

Mom was losing her short-term memory and acting more unusual, but at least she was behaving. Some of her friends at the Manor were slipping into debauchery, if one could call it that when the participants didn't really remember much anymore.

Althea, for example, had been a godly woman all her life. When she was younger, she attended a conservative Christian church, and was a strong advocate for morality and sexual abstinence among the church's teenagers. Now in her early eighties, she had severe dementia. She could still function on her own, but her mind was slipping more each month.

When Harold, another octogenarian, moved in next door to her apartment, he and Althea became friends. They'd eat meals together in the dining room and sit out on Althea's swing in the evenings. All very platonic. Then one day one of the techs came in to clean Althea's apartment only to find Althea and Harold naked from the waist down. Apparently, despite their dementia, they hadn't forgotten everything!

We later learned that such moral lapses were not uncommon among dementia patients. It wasn't that they'd suddenly become promiscuous sex machines so much as all their moral filters had diminished or disappeared completely, so there was little basis on which to decide right and wrong. "If it feels good, do it," was more than just a slogan for them. Although we found it awkward and somewhat odd, we realized that we couldn't judge the actions of men and women whose moral compasses had been destroyed by the same standards that we might judge ourselves.

Fortunately Mom refused all such temptations. She even got nervous whenever Elliot, a nattily dressed gentleman in his early nineties, sat with her and Jolene at dinner. Elliot had been an atomic scientist in Germany prior to World War II. The United States offered him asylum if he would come to America, but part of the requirements were that he be married. Elliot married a young girl he was introduced to only hours before getting on the plane, but they learned to love each other and remained married for more than fifty years, until her death. Elliot now lived alone at the Manor. A sophisticated and highly intelligent man, he loved being with Mom. He enjoyed her enthusiasm, and most of all he was intrigued by her indomitable faith.

I appreciated that Elliot was so kind and respectful to Mom. I could tell that Mom liked him too, though she'd never admit it. She regarded having feelings for another man as a betrayal of her love for my dad, who had died more than a decade earlier. We encouraged Mom to have male friends, and she enjoyed their attention, but none of them were going to get her out of her clothes!

A woman who provided assistance to residents at the Manor kept telling me, "Your mom needs a walker. She's wobbling when she walks down the hallways."

"Oh, she's fine," I responded. "She always walks that way."

"No, she's moving much more cautiously," the woman warned. "She might be a fall risk."

I thought the woman was simply trying to sell her services, but her comments concerned me, so at Mom's next appointment, Lisa asked the doctor whether he thought Mom needed a walker. "Not until it is absolutely necessary," he said. "As long as she can walk safely under her own power, I'd hold off getting her a walker."

Walk safely. That was the question: How long could she continue to walk safely under her own power? I wanted her to get some exercise, and the walk from her room to the elevator ensured that she would walk at least several hundred yards per day. At the same time, I didn't want to risk having her fall and get hurt. *Maybe we'll consider the walker soon*, I thought.

Mom believed and affirmed, " 'Prayer changes things,' just like it says in the Bible!" (That statement isn't actually in the Bible, though most of us believe the truth.)

When I attempted to correct Mom, she scoffed, "Oh, you know what I mean!"

In spiritual matters Mom may not always have been right, but she was never wrong. For instance, during my teenage years, Mom opposed the preachers who wanted to teach sex education classes to the young people of our church. With her hands on her hips, Mom declared, "I don't want my boys to study about sex. I want my boys to learn by experience!"

Thanks, Mom. We understood that she meant experience within marriage, but many of our friends did not.

Mom also was an advocate of clean underwear. "In case you are in an accident," she emphasized. I guess Mom thought that no matter how bloody or broken a person was when brought into an emergency room, the doctors and nurses were mostly concerned about the condition of the person's underwear.

Unfortunately, when it came her turn to ride in an ambulance to the hospital, she had soiled her underwear and everything else.

Chapter 18

THE TURNING POINT

In late July 2009, John and Sandie visited. Because they brought along their two dogs, they decided to stay at the Embassy Suites hotel rather than at our house. Besides, John knew how much Mom loved the water, and the hotel had a swimming pool. One day John picked up Mom and took her over to the hotel so she could spend the day with him relaxing in the pool and Jacuzzi.

They were having a grand time until Mom tried to step out of the hot tub. Her legs collapsed under her, and she tumbled back into the water. The infamous commercials proclaiming, "I've fallen and I can't get up!" became an all-too-real scenario.

It took all of John's strength and three other hotel guests who were near the hot tub to finally pull Mom out of the water. Maybe the prolonged stay in the hot water had affected Mom's heart, or perhaps had triggered another mini-stroke, but whatever happened, Mom was paralyzed in the tub, and had it not been for John and the others, she could have drowned.

The day after my family returned from vacation—Friday, July 31—I was busy returning phone calls, answering e-mails, and getting caught up. Around 11:00 a.m., I called my mom, surprised that I hadn't yet heard from her.

Mom's phone rang, but she didn't answer. I wasn't alarmed, thinking, *Okay,* The Price Is Right *is over at eleven, so perhaps she went on down to lunch early.* Although lunch was not served until noon, Mom often went to meet Jolene before going to the dining room. I didn't think it unusual that she didn't answer her phone.

By two o'clock that afternoon, I was becoming concerned. Mom wasn't answering, and normally around that time she called me. But not today. I immersed myself in work and didn't think much about Mom until nearly six o'clock, when Lisa asked, "Have you heard from your mother today?"

"Come to think of it, I haven't," I said.

"Not at all? She didn't call you?"

"No, not once."

Lisa looked at me in surprise. She knew my mom's routine of calling me a dozen times or more each day. "And you haven't called her?"

"Yeah, I did, about five or six times, but she never picked up."

"We'd better check on her." Lisa called my mom's number one more time. When she didn't answer, she called Mom's friend Jolene.

"Miss Jolene, do you know if Minnie has come down for her meals today?"

Jolene's short-term memory was nearly as bad as my mom's, but she was certain she hadn't seen Mom at any meals that day. "I'll go up and check on her." Lisa thanked Jolene and then called the Manor office. Phyllis, one of the assistant managers, answered and Lisa asked if she had seen my mom.

"No, come to think of it," Phyllis said, "I haven't seen Minnie all day long. That is unusual. I'll run right up and check on her."

"Okay, please call us back and let us know, will you?"

"Of course."

We waited a few minutes for Phyllis to call back. Meanwhile, almost instinctively, Lisa began gathering my mom's identification, social security card, and various health insurance cards. Five minutes went by and we hadn't heard from Phyllis.

"Let's go over to the Manor," I said. "If everything is okay, we'll say we just stopped by to say hello." Lisa was already moving toward the door.

When we arrived at the Manor, Phyllis came running out to meet us. She turned on her heel and walked with us back inside the building, quickly explaining that Mom had fallen and had apparently been on the floor all day in her own urine and excrement. Phyllis had gone up to check on her and found her on the floor, naked, with some underwear nearby, as though Mom was trying to get dressed. Her knee was badly bruised and bleeding slightly, but other than that she didn't seem to be cut—a serious concern since Mom's daily medicines included the blood thinner Coumadin. Phyllis called two staff members to help move Mom onto the bed, but when they lifted her to her feet, her legs were like rubber. She couldn't stand on her own, so they pulled her onto the bed and Phyllis covered her with a nightgown that she found in Mom's closet. By the time we got there, Phyllis had already called 9-1-1 and an ambulance was on the way. She and Lisa and I rushed to the elevator to go up to the third floor.

Lisa ran the length of the hallway, I walked as fast as I could, and Phyllis followed, with me calling back over my shoulder to her. The door to Mom's room was wide open, so we hurried inside. The room felt like an oven. Sabina, one of the women who assisted residents at the Manor, was tending to my mother on the bed. Sabina had opened the back door and turned on the air-conditioning to get some air flowing in the room.

Seeing my mom lying disheveled and helpless on the bed unnerved me, yet I dared not give in to my emotions. I needed to be encouraging to her. She seemed to recognize me.

"Mom, what happened? Are you okay? Are you hurting anywhere?" I asked in rapid succession, violating what I had learned about dementia, that dementia victims can handle only one question or bit of information at a time.

"I'm fine," she answered weakly. "I just fell against the air conditioner and I couldn't get up. I'm so glad you're here."

By that time the paramedics were also there, wheeling a gurney into Mom's crowded apartment.

Her apartment had three emergency cords: one in the bathroom, another in the living area, and one near her bed. Ironically, Mom had fallen or dragged herself into the center of the room. She was only a few feet away from an emergency cord, and probably less than that from her phone. Yet she neither pulled an emergency cord nor attempted to call anyone. Nor did she answer her phone when I had called throughout the day. She continued to lie on the floor all day long, possibly as much as nine to twelve hours. During that time, she couldn't get up to make her way to the bathroom, so her bowels and bladder eventually did what came naturally. I never did find out why or how she had turned the heater on full blast in July.

Later, at the hospital, I questioned Mom, but her answers made little sense. "Why didn't you pull one of the emergency cords in your room?" I asked.

"I couldn't remember what they were for," she replied.

"Didn't you hear me calling you on your phone?" I pressed.

"Yes, that phone rang off the hook all day long. But I couldn't get to it to answer it."

"Did you call out for help?"

"No," she said. "Somebody was pounding on my door earlier."

"Maybe it was one of your friends," Lisa suggested. "Why didn't you call out to ask them to help you?"

"Oh, I didn't think they could handle the situation any better than I could," she answered.

Chapter 19

A POIGNANT REMINDER

M om's geriatric doctor did not have privileges at the hospital to which Mom had been taken by the ambulance, so once out of the emergency room, Mom was placed in "critical care" and seen by the "hospitalist," a doctor who was assigned to the case similar to a lawyer being assigned to cases in which the defendant does not have legal representation. We weren't happy with that type of care, but at the time we were grateful for anyone who could help Mom.

A major disadvantage to the hospitalist, however, was that he had to procure and ascertain basic information about my mom's condition—information that her geriatric doctor already knew. That, and the fact that he didn't get around to visiting her room until nearly midnight after a long, traumatic day, made her level of cooperation and his chances of gathering accurate information far less than optimal. For nearly an hour he peppered her with a plethora of questions, and Mom patiently endured his queries. Finally the hospitalist sat back in his chair and crossed his arms.

"Well, Minnie, I've been asking you a lot of questions. Do you have any questions for me?"

"Yes," Mom replied without hesitation. "Are you a Christian?"

"No, I'm not," the doctor replied. "Actually, I'm Jewish."

"That's okay," Mom said. "God loves Jewish people too."

"I tried reading the Old Testament one time," the doctor said, "but by the time I got to Noah, it was getting so violent, I had to put it down. And I've never picked it up again."

"Well, just keep reading," Mom encouraged him. "You'll like it."

"Would you like me to be a Christian?" the doctor probed.

"Yes, I would," Mom answered.

"Why?"

"So you can go to heaven and be with Jesus."

It was a bizarre scene, with the doctor trying to determine whether Mom could comprehend abstract concepts, and my mom trying to encourage the doctor to trust in Jesus. Yet it was so "Mom." That's who she was; everything else paled in importance. What really mattered to her was a person's relationship with Jesus.

The doctor motioned for me to follow him outside Mom's room. Peering over his glasses at his clipboard, he asked me, "Does anyone in your family have a history of dementia?"

"Just my mom," I answered lightheartedly.

"Your mother has dementia?" the doctor asked. "You know that?"

"Ah, yes. Didn't you?" I couldn't believe that this doctor had grilled my exhausted mother for more than an hour in an attempt to form a diagnosis we already knew. I had a bad feeling about this guy treating her, but it was a good lesson. I couldn't assume that medical professionals caring for Mom were informed that she had dementia. I had to tell them.

The following morning when I visited Mom at the hospital, she seemed more vigorous but still could not stand. A physical therapist worked with her while we talked, but she didn't make much progress. Since dementia differs slightly from Alzheimer's in that it is a "step-down" process, rather than a direct slide, it made sense that this latest incident had dropped Mom several levels on her ability to function normally. I knew now that dementia patients rarely move back "up the ladder," but I still hoped that Mom would rally and recover to at least the point where she had been functioning at the Manor.

Later that afternoon I stopped back at the hospital and found Mom asleep. Gazing at her as she dozed in the hospital bed, I pondered, *What was I supposed to have learned from this woman? And did I learn it adequately to pass on to my own children? Did I catch the lessons, the reasons why I was born to Minnie Abraham, not Minnie Somebody Else?*

People said that Mom and I looked alike. Often, when somebody mentioned the similarity of our appearance in Mom's presence, I'd joke, "Well, that's not too good for either of us, is it?" Mom smiled knowingly. I knew she was proud of me, and I was proud to be her son. Nevertheless, for most of my lifetime prior to my dad's death, we rarely expressed love in my family. It was simply a given that we loved one another. We were especially poor at expressing "love out loud." Ironically, after Dad died, we were all more open about verbalizing the words *I love you.*

I'd missed far too many opportunities to let my mom know that I loved her. As I looked at the diminutive little lady in the hospital bed, I vowed to myself not to miss another one.

Chapter 20

REHAB WORLD

If you've never entered the unusual world of a rehabilitation center, you are missing something. "Rehab world" is a surreal existence where some people go in and come out restored, while others enter and can never leave.

The hospital kept Mom for five days before discharging her. They had no further reason to keep her, since she was walking with assistance, and her knee was well bandaged and no longer a problem. She seemed cogent enough to practice walking on her own and hopefully get back to "normal."

Rather than allowing Mom to go back to the Manor, the doctor at the hospital encouraged me to find a rehabilitation facility that would receive her. Fortunately, I was able to secure her admission to NHC Healthcare, a relatively new, impressively appointed rehabilitation center, which was literally within walking distance of Mom's home at the Manor. I signed the admission papers and waited for the ambulance to transfer her. By the time I had completed the paperwork, the paramedics were rolling Mom down the hallway on a gurney to her new room, which was similar to a hospital room, but fancier. Although I could not have known it at the time, this was an important juncture, since I was basically agreeing to keep Mom in a facility costing more than $6,000 per month! She had good insurance, as well as Medicare and a supplemental Blue Cross policy to cover medications and additional charges if she stayed more than ten days at the facility, but even with her insurance coverage, if Mom were to stay longer, we'd be out of pocket a hefty amount of cash. That was the tricky part. I had no idea how long she would stay, but I was hoping she would need only a few days of physical therapy.

At NHC two patients shared a room; Mom's roommate at the facility had undergone hip replacement and was hoping to go home soon. She was friendly enough, but I could tell that she and Mom were not going to be best friends. *That's okay,* I thought. *Mom won't be here long.*

On August 6 Mom began her therapy at NHC. The facility employed an entire staff of physical therapists, including Nathan, a handsome young man assigned to work with Mom. Nathan helped Mom exercise while Lisa and I watched, forcing ourselves not to jump in and assist her. We knew she had to relearn how to walk on her own.

Nathan said, "Now, Minnie, we're going to do some marches."

"Okay," Mom said. She rolled her eyes as if to say, "How silly."

The therapist said, "I see you rolling your eyes, Miss Minnie. Now, come on; let's march."

So she'd march, lifting her feet up and down, slowly, and always reluctantly.

The center had a piano at the far corner of the building, so after Mom and Nathan were done, I used the piano as an incentive for Mom to walk the length of the hall.

"It's a beautiful black grand piano," I told her. "You're going to love it."

She walked until she got tired, then I quickly transferred her from a walker to a wheelchair. I pushed her the remaining distance to the piano and positioned her in front of it so she could play. Sitting in the wheelchair, her feet could barely reach the piano's pedals, but her hands found the keyboard and her feeble fingertips began picking out a tune. There was a Baptist hymnal on the piano, so we found songs that Mom knew and she played them all. She'd simply ask, "What key is it in?"

"Two flats," I responded, looking at the music. And she'd start playing the song. We sang hymns for nearly an hour, Mom never reading the music, but playing them by memory. A nurse had told me that music, and especially deeply felt, spiritually oriented music, remains in the mind and is the last element to go for many dementia patients. As fascinating as that premise was to think about, I was convinced the music flowed from Mom's heart.

During Mom's first evening at the rehab center, Dr. D'Amico stopped by to check on her. She had been complaining of backaches, but worse yet, she was convinced that her closet doorknob was moving. She told the doctor so during his visit. The doctor looked at me and raised his eyebrows. I recalled our first meeting when Dr. D'Amico had told me that Mom would not get better. Now his words seemed prophetic.

Outside Mom's room the doctor and I discussed Mom's condition, including her fear of the noises in the hallway, the doorknob moving, and other disconcerting symptoms. She could have been hallucinating because of the dementia, but we deduced that the hallucinations might also be a side effect of the Dilantin (also known as phenytoin), a strong anti-seizure medicine she was receiving.

Regardless whether her fears were real or imagined, it was tough to hear her plaintive pleas.

"Ken, take me home. I don't want to stay here," she cried. "Please, I'm afraid. That doorknob keeps moving all night long."

"I want to take you home, Mom," I'd say, "but I can't take you until you can walk on your own, get to the bathroom, and take care of yourself." I didn't address the moving doorknob.

"I can do that."

"Okay, show me."

Mom tried to move her legs, but couldn't swing them over the side of the bed.

"See what I mean? I need you to eat your food, and drink lots of water so you can get strong. And when you can walk real well, I'll be glad to take you home."

"I can walk," she said.

"I know, Mom."

With my assistance Mom was able to get into a wheelchair, so I pushed her up the hallway to the snack room, where an enclosed aviary boasted numerous brightly colored birds. Mom was fascinated by the birds and enjoyed locating each one behind the glass. I hated seeing her in that wheelchair, but at least the chair made it possible for me to get her out of her room for a change of scenery.

One week dissolved into another, then another, and Mom was still at the rehab center. Any day now, I was hoping that she could return to the Manor, but the rehab workers didn't offer much hope. Quite the opposite. During our first "progress" meeting, one of the staff members asked, "Where do you plan to take Minnie when she leaves here?"

"Why, home, of course," I replied. "Where else?"

The group in the conference room looked at each other as though hoping someone else would answer the question. Finally, the nurse spoke up. "Well, you might want to begin investigating other options."

"Other options?" I had no desire to explore other options. I wanted to take my mother home and get back to normal, whatever that was.

Chapter 21

THE MEMORY UNIT

F our weeks into Mom's rehab, she was still at NHC, and her progress had stalled. The social worker from NHC left a message on my voice mail asking to meet with me. I stopped by her office the next day before I went to visit Mom. The social worker was a young woman I guessed to be in her mid-twenties who seemed friendly enough, yet gave a distinct impression that she was more concerned about her job than she was about my mom. She greeted me cordially, and turned immediately to her files.

"Mrs. Abraham is progressing quite well," she said, "and is now able to walk approximately eighty steps with the help of a walker." The young woman continued reading her files as she spoke to me. "She now qualifies to be moved out of skilled care into the memory unit."

"That's great," I responded, genuinely encouraged.

The NHC social worker presented this move as if it were a step up, that Mom "qualified" for a move. I thought that was a good thing. It wasn't. I had no comprehension of how awful placing Mom in the memory unit would be.

The memory unit at NHC was a separate enclosed area, sealed off behind observation glass and locked doors. Many of the nearly incoherent residents in the unit were heart-wrenching sights to behold. One man sat leaning over so far in a wheelchair that his knuckles literally scraped the floor. Another man had keeled over onto a card table, his face buried in a pile of magazines—apparently he had fallen asleep while reading. A woman sat at a dining table, singing and playing in her food like a two-year-old. With their heads drooping against their chests, numerous other patients were sleeping while sitting up in their chairs. For all its freshly painted walls, carpeted floors, and modern décor, the memory unit reeked of the strong smell of urine.

As soon as we entered the unit, we saw an elderly woman sitting in a wheelchair, holding a doll baby to her breast. *Oh, my,* I thought. *The dear woman is clutching on to that baby doll as though she were caring for a real baby.* I glanced around the room and noticed several other elderly women holding baby dolls as well. I guessed that the dolls were used for some sort of therapy.

Mom noticed the women with baby dolls too. She recognized that, although she wasn't hitting on all cylinders, she was more "with it" and functioning much better than most of the people in the memory unit.

"Look at that," Mom said, nodding toward a woman with a doll to her breast. "How sad."

Mom despised being there, and I hated for her to be there. Unfortunately, the social worker at NHC had transferred Mom to the unit before I really understood what the program was all about. I immediately requested that Mom be placed back in the main facility, but her bed had already been filled. She would have to remain in the memory unit for a few nights until another bed opened.

Her first night in the memory unit was not a good one. The woman in the bed next to Mom looked as though she had been in an auto accident. Her face and eyes were black, blue, and purple, not as the result of a car wreck, we were told, but from falling. She wailed loudly all through the night, making it difficult for Mom to sleep.

The second night Mom attempted to get up on her own, without assistance, even though a nurse was in the room at the time. Mom tripped over a wheelchair and hit her head on the hard tile floor. It was the first of several falls she experienced in rehab that would eventually label her as a "fall risk." Unfortunately this fall would have long-term ramifications.

Finally Mom was moved back to a "normal" rehab section—I had requested the move on Tuesday, August 25; she hit her head on August 26; we made the move on Thursday, August 27.

Each afternoon I left work early to attend therapy classes with Mom. "Therapy" is a catchall term for the incredibly difficult road back to doing even basic things—such as standing up, going to the bathroom, or taking a bath without assistance. Mom's afternoon PT included riding a stationary bike, lifting her legs while holding a volleyball between them, raising her arms, and trying to pin letters on a bulletin board. It all seemed so meaningless, but Mom dutifully did what the therapists asked.

Observing Mom folding clothes as part of her therapy was heartbreaking. She spent twenty minutes trying to smooth out the legs on a pair of sweat pants. All the while, the therapist was watching, and I was encouraging her, "That's great, Mom. I knew you could do it. You always pressed a good crease in my pants when I went to school." It struck me how demeaning this whole process was, yet so necessary, if there was any hope of Mom ever going home.

Meanwhile, there were new legal matters to consider. Dr. D'Amico and I reviewed the decisions that had to be made in case Mom was hospitalized again. We examined Mom's living will and settled on using "no extraordinary measures" to keep her artificially alive. Part of that discussion involved a "do not resuscitate order," which meant that, should Mom slip into a coma or a potentially life-ending trauma, the hospital would not hook her up to a bunch of machines, but simply allow nature to take its course. Since my faith was in God rather than "nature," I felt few qualms about signing that form.

Chapter 22

THE NURSING
HOME DECISION

When John visited Mom the weekend of August 27, her condition had degenerated. She could barely hold up her head and was nearly incoherent, not at all unlike the people in the memory unit. At one point, Mom looked over at John and said, "So this is it, huh?"

"What do you mean, Mom?"

"So this is where I wind up?"

"No, Mom. You just have to get better so we can take you home," John tried to encourage her.

Nevertheless, when John and I were not at NHC with Mom, we were out touring various assisted-living facilities and "long-term living facilities"—in other words, nursing homes. Few things in life are more painful than the decision to place a loved one in an institution. But when your parent can no longer care for himself or

131

herself, or you cannot care for him or her at home, or your loved one needs special, skilled nursing care, the choices become inevitable.

Beyond that, caring for someone with dementia or Alzheimer's takes a ghastly toll on even the best family relationships. The normal pressures of life are exacerbated exponentially when your family member needs constant attention. Such care disrupts your established patterns and routines. It requires enormous amounts of your time, money, and energy, and nearly every other relationship in life will suffer. Husbands and wives will have less time for each other and for their children, often at a period in life when you were anticipating a lessening of responsibilities and more freedom. Your business or career will take a hit, as there simply aren't enough hours in the day to get everything done and be there for Mom or Dad too.

Perhaps worse than the time and financial aspects of placing a parent in an assisted-living or a skilled-care facility is the awful sense of guilt one feels. *Isn't there any way possible that we can avoid this?* you think. *If we bend a little further, give a bit more, couldn't we continue to keep Mom or Dad at home?* The questions are endless, but the answers often point in the same direction.

Moreover, I remembered when my parents had desperately attempted to care for my Aunt Anna, who also suffered from dementia. Mom and Dad tried everything, even hiring live-in help so Aunt Anna could remain in her own home. We later discovered that the help helped themselves to many of Aunt Anna's valuable heirlooms. Between paying for live-ins and paying the high fees the nursing home charged when we were finally able to get her admitted, my parents exhausted every penny of my Aunt Anna's life savings and most of their own financial resources as well.

When my family and I finally resigned ourselves to the truth that we could not return Mom to the Manor, nor could any of us manage her at our homes, that was the easy part. Next came the awful task of finding her a suitable place to live—a decent facility with professional care at an affordable price—a tall order. The "affordable" institutions were, for the most part, poorly staffed, dirty, smelly pigpens for older people. I wish I were exaggerating. At several places where John, Lisa, or I inquired, we were astonished that the board of health granted the facilities a license to operate.

On the other hand, the squeaky-clean, quality-care, professionally staffed facilities were so expensive we wondered which would come first: Mom's funeral or the financial bankruptcy of our entire family. Furthermore, despite the exorbitant costs, the better facilities were filled to capacity and had waiting lists a mile long.

We began our search looking at both assisted-living facilities and skilled-care homes. The assisted-living places were usually more attractive, but we quickly learned that for Mom to be allowed to live there, she had to be able to get around by herself, get to meals under her own power, and basically operate much the same as she had at the Manor, with the addition of professional staff to check on her and to assist with her medications. Other than that, she was still on her own.

The nursing homes were more depressing, since most of the residents were confined to wheelchairs and required around-the-clock care. A few places combined graduated care, in which residents could move from assisted living to a skilled-care facility within the same building as their mobility decreased or the dementia increased.

The nursing home decision process was gut-wrenching, with hours spent touring facilities, meeting administrators, comparing services, observing people slumped over in wheelchairs lined up in the halls, and puzzling over the senior citizens meandering aimlessly through the buildings. At one hospital-like facility, dementia patients wore special BOLO tags, indicating "Be on the Lookout" for these people because they have dementia and may not know where they are going or why. A shocking 60 percent of the 5.4 million American Alzheimer's and dementia patients will wander away from home.[1] To help prevent patients going AWOL, many of the facilities we visited had "locked-down" sections, similar to the memory unit at NHC, where dementia and Alzheimer's patients were kept separate from the general population. It was horribly depressing to tour these areas, to see the conditions and hear the loud wails from some patients, the hysterical laughter from others, and the debilitating circumstances of so many of the senior adults. I couldn't help thinking, *This is someone's mom; that is someone's dad.*

For the most part, the staffs of the facilities appeared to be caring and compassionate, although most of the "technicians," the hospital grunt workers who lifted patients, cleaned bedpans, administered showers, and did many of the mundane tasks assigned to "hospital orderlies" in the past, seemed stressed out and overworked.

Certainly, cleanliness and quality professional medical care are top priorities when selecting a long-term care facility. We also hoped that if Mom had to be in such a place, it would be open to Bible studies, Christian music, and speakers. Proximity to our home was also a factor, since I knew Mom would not do well someplace where we could visit only occasionally.

Often the decision comes down to money. Premium assisted-living and skilled-care homes currently range between $3,000 to more than $6,000 a month, and that doesn't include disposable diapers! Unless you prepare in advance, these kinds of expenses can bust even the best budget. Mom did not have a "long-term" health insurance policy, and her Blue Cross policy, for which she had sacrificially and faithfully paid for years, did not cover the entire amount of her care, even with the US government's Medicare program paying the lion's share of the long-term care expenses.

Our only hope was Medicaid, but to qualify for that assistance, Mom could not own more than $2,000 in total assets. In a matter of days, we would have to make difficult decisions regarding Mom's limited resources, draining her bank account by spending her money on things we knew she would eventually need, including clothes, and yes, disposable adult diapers. One of the expenses allowed by the government was a prepaid funeral, so we explored that option and found a company that not only could help us arrange for the ceremony but also allowed advance payment for everything from the flowers on the casket to a meal for mourners after the interment. It felt horribly morbid, and almost underhanded, determining the details of Mom's final demise while she was still living, but we felt it would be far better to deal with such matters earlier, rather than waiting until the last minute.

One of the last long-term care facilities we toured was Grace Healthcare, an older, much smaller complex located in our community, and housing only about eighty patients. We almost ignored it because of its age, but then someone told us that it had been newly renovated and deserved a look. The moment we walked in the door, we were impressed. For one thing, Grace did not have that ubiquitous "nursing home smell," an incessant, sour combination of urine and cleaning agents that seems to bombard your nostrils and permeate your clothes after visiting for only a matter of minutes. Quite the opposite, Grace smelled and looked clean and neat. It was brightly lit, pleasantly decorated, albeit not fancy, with framed black-and-white photographs of familiar celebrities from the 1940s decking the walls. Best of all, Glenda, the admissions director, informed us that Grace had just recently acquired the services of a new medical director—Dr. Stephen D'Amico, Mom's geriatric doctor. We were sold.

There was only one problem: Mom had only a few days left of skilled-care coverage by her insurance. If we were not able to move her to Grace quickly, within the skilled-care coverage period, she'd have to go on a waiting list with hundreds of Medicaid patients in front of her.

Although we were ecstatic about the possibility of getting Mom into Grace, we knew that if she didn't rally soon, the move might not be necessary. Mom continued to go downhill. One night she was so bad we thought she was going to die. While Mom lay motionless, I read a long passage from Psalm 119 and several other passages as John and Lisa listened and prayed for her. By the time John left Nashville, he was convinced that Mom would not last much longer, and had we not discovered that she was on some harmful drugs, he probably would have been right.

Chapter 23

. . . .

MONITOR MEDICATIONS

I f there is a cardinal rule for caregivers of loved ones afflicted with dementia or Alzheimer's, it must be: Monitor medicines closely! We didn't at first. Like most trusting, compliant family members, we assumed the medical professionals caring for Mom were giving her medications that she needed. Regarding pain medication, we thought they were giving her Tylenol, but in fact they were giving her hydrocodone, a highly addictive narcotic that produces euphoria similar to heroin or morphine, along with Lortab, Vicodin, and other medications. And for what? A skinned knee?

Consequently, Mom was perpetually sleepy, lethargic, uncooperative, unable to perform menial tasks—all of which was duly noted by her therapists—but nobody noted that she was knocked out by the drugs! No doubt the administration of pain medication is a delicate and debatable matter among caregivers of dementia patients, but I wondered if much of the medication given is simply to keep the patient quiet and less troublesome. It seemed that way in Mom's case. Moreover, she had dementia! When asked if she was in pain, she may have been hurting, but more than likely she was not. Even when she claimed to be in pain, it was difficult to tell if it was real or imagined. She may have been recalling a pain from fifty years previously. Yet the nurses continued to take Mom's word as gospel.

"Do you hurt anywhere, Mrs. Abraham?" a well-meaning nurse might ask.

Mom always answered, "Yes, I hurt all over."

"Would you like a pain pill?"

"Oh, yes, please." So every few hours another nurse loaded Mom with more strong meds. Besides sending her into a non-functioning, disoriented blur, the worst result of the medication was that Mom would not eat. I took her in a wheelchair to the lovely restaurant-style dining area at NHC, ordered her food, and then watched in despair as Mom missed her mouth with her spoon, or could not get a glass of juice to her lips without spilling it all over herself. Her head drooped lower and lower and she looked as though she was going to fall face forward right into her food. I tried feeding her, but her mouth refused to move. Each meal was more discouraging than the previous one.

One night around 9:00 p.m., just after Lisa and I prayed with my mom and were about to leave, a nurse popped her head into Mom's room, and asked, "Mrs. Abraham, would you like your pain pill tonight?"

"Oh, yes, thank you," Mom replied.

"What pain pill?" Lisa asked, ignoring Mom's response and looking directly at the nurse.

"Well, let's see, she gets several," the nurse answered cheerily as she flipped some pages on a clipboard chart.

"For what?" Lisa asked.

"For her back, her leg," the nurse read from the chart.

"Are you kidding?" Lisa pressed. "Can I see that? Let's step outside." Lisa and the nurse left the room, and I could hear Lisa excoriating her in the hallway.

When she returned Lisa was livid. "You aren't going to believe what they've been giving her," she said to me. I didn't have time to answer before Lisa launched into a list of the strong pain medications that Mom was receiving, none of which she actually needed and some of which had been prescribed initially, the day of her fall, and were still on her chart.

"You'll have to call Dr. D'Amico tomorrow," Lisa said, "since the nurse is not authorized to take your mom off the pain pills, only a doctor. No wonder Grandma Minnie seems so lethargic; she's hooked on drugs!"

First thing in the morning, I called Dr. D'Amico, and told him about the medications. He met me at NHC and wrote an order in Mom's charts to slowly wean her off the strong painkillers. She had literally become addicted to prescription pain meds, and now she had to be slowly and carefully backed down from them. It was ridiculous. But we learned through that situation that we could not count on anyone else to monitor Mom's medications. We had to control what she received, even from health-care professionals.

Thankfully she began to rouse a bit once the caregivers ceased to dope her down. It took several days before Mom was back to her usual upbeat personality. She still couldn't walk without assistance, but she was no longer groveling in her food or sleeping all day. Again hope surged in me that maybe, just maybe, she might get stronger and be able to function somewhat normally again.

On Thursday, September 10, Lisa and I donned Tennessee Titans sweatshirts and went to visit Mom and watch the NFL's opening night game between the Titans and Mom's Pittsburgh Steelers.

Back in December 2008, when Mom was still in good health, we had taken her to the Steelers-Titans showdown in Nashville on one of the coldest days of the year. The Titans were on their way to the NFL's best record that season, and the Steelers were on their way to the Super Bowl, so procuring tickets to what was sure to be one of the best games of the year was a challenge, but our friend Bob Kernodle found someone willing to sell four tickets to us. On game day Mom, Lisa, and Alyssa went out for breakfast, then layered ski clothes on Mom while I taught Sunday school. As soon as I finished, we hopped in the car and raced to a special parking area close to the stadium, but which was still a long walk in thirteen-degree temperatures.

"Come on, Mom. Let's walk as fast as we can," I pumped her up as we stepped out of the warm car into the frigid air.

Despite frigid temperatures, Mom said, "It was
a good game. Too bad our boys lost."

"I'll do my best," she replied from somewhere inside her ski clothes. Wrapped like mummies, Alyssa, Lisa, and I locked our arms with Mom's and literally dragged her the distance from the parking lot to the stadium. Huffing and puffing, breathing through scarves, we finally made it to the ticket turnstiles, only to discover that our seats were in the far end zone. We paused long enough for Mom to go to the restroom, a major undertaking considering all the clothes she was wearing, and we made it to our seats just before kickoff.

Living up to all the hype, the game was a bone-crunching display of football, with the Titans delivering a definitive beating to the Steelers, defeating them 31-14. We lingered a few minutes to take some pictures after the game was over.

"How did you like the game, Mom?" I asked.

"It was a good game," she said, barely moving her nearly frozen lips. "Too bad our boys lost."

Now, loaded with Mom's favorite munchies and soda pop from home, Lisa and I were once again taking Mom to see the Steelers, but this time, barely ten months later, she was in a wheelchair and unable to walk more than a few steps, let alone the distance from the parking lot to the stadium. We parked Mom in front of the television set and called my brothers in Florida to let them know that Mom was tracking along with the game. We enjoyed the Titans-Steelers rematch, but not even a Steelers' victory could assuage Mom's sadness that she could not go home with us that night. This was our new normal.

It took two weeks before we could make the switch from NHC to Grace. The delays cost us more than $5,500.

Transporting Mom from NHC to Grace was an adventure in itself. Lisa dressed Mom in a nice outfit, and after an exasperating two-hour wait at NHC because the paperwork was not ready, I finally wheeled Mom out the hallway to our car.

Getting Mom into the vehicle when she could barely get out of the wheelchair, much less stand or flex her body, was a trick indeed. Lisa and I twisted, turned, and maneuvered her until she finally plopped into the backseat of the car.

When at last we were ready, the rear seat belt holding my mother into an awkward slouching position, I looked in the rearview mirror and said, "Hold on tight. Here we go."

Mom didn't mind. "Oh, Ken, thank you so much for getting me out of that place. I am so thankful to be leaving." She repeated several similar statements, and then it struck me: *She thinks I'm taking her home!*

Although I had told her that we were transferring her to the facility where Dr. D'Amico was the head medical director, that information didn't connect in Mom's brain. She thought this effort was all to get her back to the Manor. Instead I was delivering her to a nursing home. I felt like a total cad.

Chapter 24

GRACELAND

D ementia patients dislike anything that disrupts their routine, so I shouldn't have been surprised that checking her into her new room at Grace sent Mom into a dither. She was to room with Naomi, an elderly woman who had suffered a severe stroke and a broken hip. Naomi could understand fairly well when someone spoke to her, but she communicated with great difficulty.

Mom didn't want to stay there.

I pushed Mom in a wheelchair, easing around the facility, helping her to get familiar with her new location. We toured the hallways, and stopped off in the Family Room, a small sitting area with a television and phone, where visiting family members could come apart from the main population. Then we went to the dining room, which also served as an activities room. I pointed out a piano in the corner, and Mom's eyes brightened. A number of residents were watching television, while others sat at tables, waiting for dinner to be served. Almost all of the residents were confined to wheelchairs.

"I don't want to stay here," Mom said to me.

"Why, Mom?"

She leaned up toward me, and whispered, "A lot of these people have lice!"

"No they don't!" I laughed. "They look pretty good to me."

Mom's skin wasn't doing so well herself. Her legs looked dry and the skin flaked off at a touch. Lisa helped her use a cream hair removal product and then coated her legs in body lotion. Mom loved it.

"Feel how soft my legs are!" she gushed over and over like a child, raising her pant leg up to her shin to show me.

"That's great, Mom. Put your pant legs down, please."

In the activities room we gathered around the piano and found an old "Singspiration" songbook with a lot of gospel songs that Mom knew by heart. I'd call out the songs and she'd play them by memory, with me making feeble attempts to sing along. As I did, I heard her weak voice singing the harmony part. I bit my lip to hide my emotions and kept right on singing. After a while the cleaning lady came in to the dining room, so I had Mom play one more number, "How Great Thou Art," and I drew her wheelchair away from the piano and took her back to her room.

I stood outside Mom's room as the techs helped her get ready for bed. When the nurses exited Mom's room, I went inside and found Mom tucked under the sheet and cover, and her bed low-ered to just inches off the floor. On the floor, next to her bed, lay a large blue pad, similar to the mats on which we used to wrestle in high school physical education classes. With Mom as a fall risk, the nurses were taking no chances.

I knelt down on the mat next to Mom's bed and took her hand in mine. "I'm going to go home and do some work," I told her.

"You get some rest and I'll see you in the morning." Instantly, I could see the fear leap into Mom's eyes.

"No, Ken," she begged. "Please don't leave me here. Take me with you."

"I can't, Mom. I can't carry you, and you can't walk yet."

"I can walk."

"Not well enough to make it up the stairs at our house," I answered.

"Don't leave me." Tears welled in my mother's eyes, and my heart responded commensurately. "Stay here," she pleaded. "You can put a sleeping bag right there on the floor. I won't mind."

I hated this new life we were forced to experience. As compassionate and helpful as everyone at Grace had been, and as smoothly as the transition had been made, my mom was now housed in a nursing home, and no matter what sugary-sounding name they gave it—skilled care, long-term care facility, whatever—it was still a nursing home, a last resort from which she would most likely never return.

I had told my brother earlier that day, "The toughest part of all this is that you know when she leaves this place, she's coming out on a gurney." He agreed.

"I have to go do some work, Mom," I said. "I've been here with you all day, and I just haven't gotten any writing done."

"Oh, okay," she replied quickly, as though she was content to relinquish me to my work. That was okay. To go home to my family, or even to sit down and have a sandwich and watch a ball game would have not been reason enough to return home that night. But for me to go home to work was much more acceptable to her.

We prayed together, as would become our habit, with me kneeling on the mat by her bed, holding her hand. When I completed my prayer, Mom continued with hers, going on for another five minutes before closing, "In Jesus' precious name, Amen."

The following day, I drove to Grace to have lunch with Mom. Sitting at a table in the activities room with a group of elderly women, all of whom were dementia and Alzheimer's patients, Mom smiled at the women pleasantly, then turned to me and said under her breath, "Get me out of this place. Today!"

"I can't do that until you can walk out of here," I said quietly, falling back on my default excuse for not taking her back to her home or mine.

After lunch was therapy time. The therapist dumped a laundry basket full of washcloths on the table in the activity room. The residents went to work folding them. Besides keeping them busy, folding washcloths is an activity to help dementia patients use their fingers and hands, folding and smoothing out the washcloths, stacking them on the table. They seem to know that it is an endless job, but they willingly participate. One elderly woman said, "We fold these same washcloths every day." Another one chimed in, "Yes, and we don't even use them!"

Mom realized that it was an exercise in futility, so I kept reminding her that the therapist was getting her ready for activities she'd need to do at home, once she got there. Although in the pit of my stomach, barring a miracle from God, I knew Mom would never need this skill again. But I believed in miracles.

Many residents at Grace lived with some form of dementia or Alzheimer's and were on an inexorable, irreversible downward slide. One fascinating couple, however, seemed different than the other residents.

Joe and Mary were always seen together, with Joe patiently and lovingly guiding Mary through the halls. Later we learned that Mary suffered from Alzheimer's and could no longer care for herself; Joe, however, was perfectly healthy and mentally alert. He had sacrificially left their home and moved in at Grace to live with his wife and help care for her. What love!

Another woman, Mrs. Jones, called out to all the men who passed by her doorway. "Arthur!" she'd yell sternly. "Arthur, where are you going? You come back here right now!" Her husband, I discovered, had died three years earlier, and she missed him fiercely.

One day when I visited, I noticed Mrs. Jones weeping and calling out for Arthur. I went to her, gently placed my hand on her shoulder, and said, "It's okay, Mrs. Jones. I'm glad to see you today." She calmed down, and smiled warmly. From that day on, every time I visited my mom, I'd stop to say hello to Mrs. Jones. Once I called out to her, "Hello, Mrs. Jones! You certainly look beautiful today."

Mrs. Jones sat up straight in her wheelchair and said, "You better behave, young man. I'm married, you know."

Then there was Wanda, a large lady in her late seventies who reminded me a bit of a bulldog. She was always trying to get out of her wheelchair. A lot of people thought she was mean, so I greeted her with a big smile every time I saw her.

"Hey!" she'd call out to me as I walked toward Mom's room.

"Hi, Wanda," I said cheerily. "How are you? What can I do for you?"

"Get me a Bud."

"A Bud? What will you do with it?" I asked naively.

"I'm going to drink it!"

"Oh, I see," I said with a laugh. "I don't have any beer. Is there anything else I can do for you?"

"Take me home," Wanda demanded. "Take me to bed."

The nurses laughed as my face turned red. I quickly learned that my questions were inappropriate in a nursing home, and I changed my tact to declarative affirmations such as, "Nice to see you today."

"Seniors Gone Wild," one of the nurses joked when I told her that Wanda was seminaked again.

About a week or two into Mom's transition, she told me about seeing Dr. D'Amico at Grace.

"He's a really nice man," Mom said. "I told him that I'm living here now."

Mom's tacit acknowledgment that she was now living at a nursing home saddened me deeply. The words, "I'm living here now," were especially poignant.

In the hospital and rehab facility, Mom tended toward frustration more than self-pity. She despaired that she could not walk on her own; she couldn't get up to greet anyone who came in the room, she couldn't answer the phone (or perhaps forgot how to), and her fingertips would not function well enough to open the numerous get-well cards she received. More demeaning in her estimation, she could no longer give herself a bath and had to allow orderlies or techs to help her to the bathroom, and to wash even her private areas, which they did with great vigor, much to Mom's dismay. Even rolling over or sliding up in bed proved to be a chore.

Now at Grace, Mom's frustrations multiplied. Eating while in a wheelchair seemed an especially laborious task as Mom would chase a piece of chicken around the plate with her fork, trying to spear enough to eat.

"Here, let me help you," I suggested, cutting her food into tiny chunks.

"I can get it," she said.

"I know, but your food is getting cold," I smiled. "You're going to starve to death if you don't let me help you." I continued cutting the chicken. Mom closed her eyes and leaned back in her wheelchair. The irony hit me that my mom probably used to cut chicken for me, much as I was now cutting the food for her.

Watching her try to drink some cranberry juice was an exercise in patience for both of us—Mom holding the glass in her shaking hands, spilling the juice on her blouse, determined to find her lips and get some of the cool red liquid into her mouth. It was tempting for me to reach out and grab the glass and hold it to her lips, but I knew she had to do this for herself.

She managed a few sips of juice before the frustration overtook her. She put the glass down and went back to chasing the chicken around her plate.

Many of the residents at Grace sat in the hallways all day long, looking forlorn, longing for someone to talk with them. Of course the staff did their best to notice each person, but that wasn't the same as a visit by a child, grandchild, or friend. Some of the residents rarely had visitors, not even on weekends, and a few received no visitors at all. I felt so sorry for the grandmas and grandpas who went day after day never seeing a family member or friend. I tried to take extra time with the residents that I knew had no outside visitors. Just looking in a person's eyes, greeting him or her by name, smiling, touching a hand or a shoulder seemed to make such a difference for them.

Grace provided a number of information sessions, but few relatives attended. One seminar featured Dr. D'Amico, a highly regarded expert in his field, and twelve people showed up. Half of them were staff members. Sadly, for some people afflicted with dementia, there is a disconnect on the part of family members once the relative is safely "installed" at the nursing home.

In addition to learning the names of Mom's fellow residents, I tried to learn the names of the caregivers, the nurses, techs, and volunteers. I wanted them to know me, but more importantly, in case of problems, or if Mom did not receive proper care, I wanted them to realize that I knew them by name. Most of the caregivers we had encountered thus far in Mom's journey into dementia were patient, kind, and compassionate, with amazing attitudes and an unceasing willingness to serve. And we were grateful for each and every one of them. But the truth is not everyone serving the elderly is trustworthy. We were always watchful because some were mean, inconsiderate, deceitful, and lazy. A few had even been thieves.

Mom had no shortage of visitors. Numerous friends from our Sunday school class stopped to see Mom.

Longtime family friends Linda Gardner and her daughters drove all the way from Pennsylvania to visit my Mom. Seeing them lifted Mom's spirits, so while she spent time with them, I slipped out to see if anyone was in the activities room, where the piano was located. On my way down the hall, Glenda, the home director, saw me and called me into her office. Glenda was laughing as she said, "I want you to hear something."

"Ah . . . okay," I replied, trying to imagine what Glenda might want me to hear. Glenda punched the keys on her phone and played a voice mail from Mom in which she said, "I'm here at Graceland, and I'm trying to find my brother." Glenda chuckled at Mom's reference to Graceland, the former home of Elvis Presley. Mom's current home, of course, was Grace Healthcare, and her brother had been dead for more than thirty years. Like so many things about Mom's life these days, the message was simultaneously funny and sad.

I gathered Mom and her guests into the activities room and pushed her wheelchair up to the keyboard. "What do you want to hear, Linda?" I asked.

"I love 'How Great Thou Art,'" Linda responded. Without a bit of hesitation, Mom placed her hands on the keyboard and began the song. Linda and her daughters sang as Mom played piano and sang the harmony part. Brenda, an activities director, joined us, and led a spontaneous concert.

Using their arms and feet to pull their wheelchairs up close, residents and their guests gathered around the piano. Many of the residents who could not even carry on a conversation were mouthing the words to the old hymns. A gray-haired woman with an oxygen tank and two tubes running to her nostrils pulled her wheelchair up as close as possible to where Mom was playing the piano and a group of us were singing. I smiled at her, and her eyes brightened. Then, as Mom launched into the song, "What a Friend We Have in Jesus," the woman's eyes welled with tears, and her lips mouthed the words as she tried to sing along.

Maybe music really is the last thing to go.

Chapter 25

STAYING CONNECTED

The sense of being displaced and disconnected contributes to the confusion dementia patients experience. Mom had now been away from home for nearly ten years, and although she had lived in a nice condo in Florida, a lovely apartment in Tennessee, and even a beautiful rehab facility after her fall in 2009, she was nonetheless disconnected. That sense of being displaced and detached from everything she had known for much of her life was disturbing, and as much as she may have appreciated her new digs, her former life had vanished and she was now a nomad of sorts. "Graceland" was now her home.

While visiting with Mom in her room one night, I leaned forward and held her hand. For once her fingers were warm; in recent months her fingertips were ice-cold. Mom looked at me sadly and said, "I never thought I'd be in this situation, not able to take care of myself. I don't want to be a burden on you. Maybe I should get a job."

I didn't know whether to laugh or cry. That she even worried about being a burden on me touched me deeply; that she thought she could hold a job of course was ludicrous.

"We're glad that you are here and that we can take care of you."

Holding Mom's hand while we prayed each night reminded me of the importance of physical contact for her. Such expressions have always been awkward for me, but I realized that Mom was longing for human touch. I guess we all are. Ironically, because of the way the elderly treat each other, they rarely touch. Without touch from me, Mom could go a day to a week without any meaningful physical contact other than a nurse or orderly helping her to wipe up after going to the bathroom. It was difficult for me at first, but I forced myself to overcome my own uneasiness and reached out and held Mom's hand during visits, and especially during prayer times.

We wanted to have a birthday party for my mom in October, but because of Medicaid rules, we decided to postpone it until November, after she was officially qualified for Medicaid. Otherwise, if we had taken her out of Grace, and she had fallen, we would have been totally responsible for any hospital care or other rehabilitation she might need. Although Mom had Blue Cross insurance, it wasn't worth risking an enormous, unnecessary expense.

When my brother John called and said that he'd be coming to visit Mom in November, Lisa convinced me that it might be our last chance to have another "Minnie's hymn-sing" birthday party. At her previous sing-along birthday party, Mom was still coherent and was merely beginning to experience the effects of dementia. We wanted to do a similar party, but worried that Mom might not be able to negotiate the steps getting into our home, so we rented a room at our church for Mom's birthday party, which we celebrated in November rather than on her actual birthday of

October 7. Realistically, we knew Mom would not know or care what the date was.

We arranged to have Mom's hair done at Grace the afternoon prior to the party, and we picked out an outfit for her to wear. Lisa pinned a note to the outfit so the nurses would know that Mom was not in charge of wardrobe that day. No telling what color combinations she might have selected.

John and I left an hour early to pick her up at Grace. There we found Mom ready and sitting in a wheelchair. She looked sensational, classy and sophisticated, in her black slacks and shoes, a black turtleneck blouse, and a bright red jacket that we had picked out for her to wear. She complained about having to dress up, but when we got her wheelchair to the car, she suddenly brightened, as she realized that she was going along with us. John and I carefully helped Mom to stand and then inched her into the backseat.

At the church we eased her into another wheelchair that we had brought along, and up an elevator to where a crowd of eighty-eight people had shown up to celebrate with Mom. It was amazing. We had asked each person to wear a name tag, not so they would know each other, but so Mom could better recognize them, and the idea worked well. "Do you remember Vickie Riley?" I'd ask, pointing to Vickie's name tag.

"Oh, of course I remember Vickie," Mom replied. I smiled at Vickie, both of us knowing that Mom had received a helpful hint by glancing at the name tag. The greetings went much the same with everyone else, Mom assuring each person that she was so glad to see them again, and each person so graciously and kindly hugging Mom and making her feel special. Our friend Tommy Quinn photographed Mom with every person who came through the impromptu receiving line.

After a time of greeting and eating (a simple menu of chili, one of Mom's favorites, and cake and ice cream, of course), we moved

Mom's wheelchair over to the large grand piano. Then we invited people to call out their favorite hymns and we'd sing them. Mom didn't have a hymnbook or any other piece of music, but she played every hymn the folks called out. Several of the people in our group were professional singers or musicians, so I asked them to join us around the piano. Before long we had a fair-sounding choir. We sang for more than an hour, with Mom fielding requests. At one point, she looked up from the piano and said, "I'm going to praise my God forever!"

"Never better!"

Fresh on the heels of our successful birthday party, Lisa and I considered an even more risky adventure. We couldn't bear the thought of my mom staying in her room on Thanksgiving, so we decided to bring her to our home for the day. The nurses didn't know that I planned to take her out, so when I arrived at Grace, Mom was dressed casually, with evidence of food spattered on her sweater, but I didn't mind. I managed to get her into the car by myself and started driving through the countryside toward our home. For a few minutes it felt like old times, with my mom conversing naturally about how beautifully the leaves had changed colors. When we arrived at our home, my daughter's boyfriend and I helped Mom climb the thirty stairs to our front door. It took some time, but she made it.

Early afternoon Mom said to me, "I'm really tired. Are you taking me home soon?"

That was different. In better times, Mom rarely wanted to leave. She stayed until the kids were ready to go to bed. But now her energy levels were much lower and she tuckered out much sooner.

"We'll be going back soon," I assured her. "Just sit on the couch until we're ready to go."

We played games, and Mom made funny remarks. But all too soon, she was ready to go "home"—home to Graceland and her new banal existence.

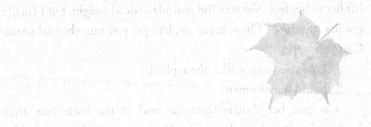

Chapter 26

RELATIVE "TRUTH"

An adult male should not have to change his mother's diapers, but I soon discovered that, like it or not, helping Mom in the bathroom was part of my new job description.

"I have to pee," Mom informed me, as we sat together on her bed at Grace.

"Okay, hang on, Mom," I said, already heading toward the hallway. "I'll get a nurse to help you." I looked out the doorway into the hall, where a nurse was usually stationed, but there was nobody to be seen.

"Oh, I'm going in my pants," I heard Mom saying, as she tried to get up.

"No!" I nearly yelled. "Don't do that." I stepped back inside her room. "Come on, I'll help you."

"Too late," she said with an impish smile. "But I think I have to do more—from the other end."

"Oh, no!" I put my arms under my mom's arms and tried to

lift her to her feet. She was 168 pounds of dead weight, but I finally got her standing. "Okay, come on, let's get you into the bathroom. Can you walk?"

"Of course I can walk," she replied.

I should have known.

I helped her shuffle from her bed to the bathroom, then knelt and pulled down her slacks. For a moment, I thought, *How demeaning this is for my mother, to have her son removing her pants.* But Mom didn't seem to mind. In fact, she seemed to have lost all inhibitions. "Oh, there's more coming!" I heard her say above me.

Oh, boy, what do I do now? There was only one thing to do. Down with her underwear and get her onto the pot as soon as possible. Her bum hit the toilet seat just in the nick of time. Another second or two and I would have been changing my own clothes.

"I'll just wait outside," I said, as sounds and smells of my mom's flatulence filled the tiny bathroom. "Call me when you are done, and I'll come back in to help you."

"Okay, thanks," Mom replied as though I had just told her that I was putting some groceries in the cupboard. I quickly closed the door.

"I'm here if you have any problems," I spoke into the door.

Mom grunted some sort of response.

I leaned my head against the door and closed my eyes. This was like taking care of a baby, only worse.

One night during the Christmas season, I stopped to see Mom, and couldn't find her. Most of the residents were sitting in the activities room awaiting a program by some Christmas carolers from a local church. From the back of the room, my eyes scanned the group sitting in their wheelchairs in a semicircle, and I didn't see Mom among them. I walked to her room, expecting to find her watching television, but when I got there, the room was empty. *That's odd,* I thought. *Where could she have gone?* I went back to the activities room, and worked my way around to the front of the residents. Then I saw her. Mom was sitting up front, and I realized why I had missed her.

She looked just like everybody else. Sitting upright and motionless in a wheelchair, staring straight ahead with a blank expression on her face, Mom blended in with the residents who had been there much longer than Mom's three and a half months. A wrenching sadness came over me as I realized afresh that Mom's condition was not improving and her mental capabilities were dwindling each day.

Beside her sat Sam, a lonely, autistic, forty-something man, always dressed in blue jeans and several layers of shirts. Sam was able to walk without assistance, so he wandered freely throughout the building. Sam especially enjoyed being around Mom, and she had taken him under her wing as a buddy.

The Christmas carolers introduced themselves and began singing. The group included a few adults, but mostly children around ten years of age. They sang enthusiastically, if not accurately hitting the notes. When they finished their first number, I was about to applaud, but noticed that nobody else in the room was clapping, not even my mom. So I stifled my response.

The singers did their best, encouraging the residents to sing along, and some—like my mom and Sam—actually did. Others mouthed some of the words to the more familiar carols.

Sam especially enjoyed the music, singing loudly and so horribly off-key that I wondered how the kids up front could keep a straight face. A few of them didn't, but most did their best to stay on pitch, no easy accomplishment with Sam's blaring intonations.

This is everyday life for my mom, I thought. *No wonder she gets depressed.*

When the carolers finished singing, I hurried to their leader to thank her for bringing the group to Grace. I wanted them to know that their efforts were appreciated and not in vain. Mom and Sam enjoyed them, if nobody else.

I pulled up a chair in front of Mom's wheelchair. "Hey, wasn't that great?" I enthused. "Did you enjoy that?"

"Oh, yes," she replied with a sleepy nod.

"They sang pretty well, didn't they?"

"Did they?" she quipped. I knew Mom noticed the off-key notes by some of the adults as well as the children, but it wasn't really fair to judge since she had Sam singing in her left ear.

We sat in the activities room for a while and talked as the techs returned the other residents to their rooms. I could tell Mom was in a bit of a funk.

"What's wrong, Mom?"

"I haven't been able to get out to buy one Christmas gift for anyone," she said sadly.

"Oh, that's okay. We all have everything we need. Besides, you can give the girls some of the stuffed animals you have in your drawer." Several church groups had visited Grace and had given plush stuffed animals as gifts to each of the residents. Mom had a penguin and a soft white puppy. Each time I visited, she told me, "Take these home for Kellee."

My niece, Kellee, lives in Florida, but Mom thought Kellee was merely a few miles away.

"You can give them to Kellee when she comes to visit," I told Mom.

"Okay, that's a good idea," she said with a smile.

On Christmas day I transported Mom to our home to celebrate the birth of Christ, and to enjoy Christmas dinner with the family. We even had some special presents made up as though she had purchased them for the kids. Later that evening we went to visit longtime friends Judy Nelon and her family.

Judy, too, had special presents for each of us, including my mom. Mom raved about Judy's kindness as she opened each present with care. Then, as if there always had to be a reminder of the dementia, even on Christmas, she looked at Judy and said, "You shouldn't have done all this for my birthday. We don't celebrate anybody else's birthday like this."

Alyssa came home from college over the Christmas holiday and stopped in to visit her grandmother. While she was there, John called from Florida, so Alyssa handed Mom the phone. Mom talked with John for about fifteen minutes. A few hours later, I arrived at Grace. Mom and I had a cup of coffee and we talked about Alyssa. Knowing that she had also talked with John, I asked, "And how is John doing?"

Mom looked back at me quizzically. "John?" she twisted her lip. "I haven't heard from John in months!"

Of course I knew better. My brother had visited on at least four occasions within recent months, and had stayed for several days each trip. He called her regularly, sometimes more than once in the same day. But Mom did not remember the conversation she'd had with him a few hours previously. That was an important lesson for me to learn in dealing with Mom's dementia—namely, she may say something totally false that she believed to be true. If I took her words at face value, I would think that my brothers neither visited nor called.

While such minor distortions didn't matter most of the time, the wrong information could be dangerous if the nurses and technicians weren't aware that Mom wasn't always the most accurate source of information about herself.

"Miss Minnie, did you take your medicine, and did you have your shower today?"

"Oh, yes, I took all my medicine, and I'm clean as a whistle," she might reply. In fact, she hadn't received her medicine that day and hadn't been near the bathtub all week. Exacerbating matters further, Mom was more cogent than many other residents at Grace. She could carry on a conversation, talk about current events she'd seen on television, make observations about other people, and she sounded quite convincing to anyone unaware of Mom's true condition.

"I'm leaving this place this afternoon," she told one of the techs one day. That wasn't unusual. What was unusual was the tech was so convinced that Mom was checking out she called me to see what time I wanted her to have my mother ready for departure.

"She's not going anywhere," I said.

"She's not? She told me that she was moving back to Pennsylvania."

"Not a chance," I answered with a laugh.

I was only glad that Mom hadn't told her she was going out nightclubbing.

One day Mom called me, a significant accomplishment since she did not have a phone in her room. But one of the nurses had taken her to the phone in the family room and helped her dial my number. I was surprised to hear from Mom, but even more surprised when she said, "Ken, last night some big, tall fellow came in my room and asked me out on a date."

"He did!" I decided to play along.

"Yes, he did," Mom replied somewhat angrily.

"Well, did you go?"

"Absolutely not!"

"Why not?"

"He wanted me to come over to his house."

"Oh, no; we'll have none of that sort of thing." I could almost see my mom nodding her head on the other end of the line.

"That's right. These men here only want one thing."

"Really? What's that?" I asked. Images of several of the men at Grace flitted across my mind. Not a virile man among them.

"You know!" Mom said.

"Oh," I tried to sound shocked. "Well, I'll have a word with him when I come over."

"Yes, that's a good idea," she said. "But hurry."

I assumed that Mom was having another of her many hallucinatory days and that she would forget all about the man in her room, but when I stopped in to visit the next day, she again brought up the subject. Sitting at the dining table with her friends Dorothy and Henrietta, Mom launched into an even more descriptive version of the man in the room story. This time there were three men courting her.

"They all want to date me," she told her wide-eyed friends. Dorothy and Henrietta giggled like schoolgirls.

"Which one wants to date you?" Dorothy asked, looking across the room at four men sitting at another dining table. Two of the four looked as though they were asleep in their wheelchairs, and the other two men had tipped their heads forward so far their noses nearly touched their chests.

"All of them," Mom replied. "They all want me."

"Oooh!" Henrietta squealed. "Will you go out with one of them?"

"No way," Mom said matter-of-factly. "He wants me to come to his house with him, and I'm not that kind of girl."

"Well, I am!" Dorothy said, her eyes dancing with excitement.

Mom gave Dorothy a dirty look, but didn't reply to her comment. Instead she upped the ante. "That good-looking man wants to come over to my house, but I told him no."

Henrietta and Dorothy sighed dreamily like teenagers in love.

The concept of "my house" was both good and bad for Mom. I was glad that she was becoming comfortable with the idea that she actually lived in her tiny room, smaller than most modern hospital rooms. The bad part was that she had taken ownership of the room, even though she had a roommate.

Naomi shared the small living area with Mom. The room was cramped already with two beds, two chests of drawers, two tray tables, two sitting chairs, and two nightstands, but when Naomi's and Mom's wheelchairs and walkers were in the room, it became an almost impassable obstacle course. Nevertheless, we put up some of the favorite pictures from Mom's former apartment at the Manor, including the large picture of Jesus with His hands outstretched that we had hung over Mom's bed to help calm her fears. The small room at Grace had become home for Mom. That was the good part. The bad news was that, like many dementia patients, she became possessive.

One day a nurse told me that Mom and Naomi had been fighting, arguing loudly and vehemently.

"Why, what's going on?" I asked.

"It seems that Naomi has not paid your mom any rent for using her portion of the room," the nurse said with a smile. "Naomi is living in your mom's home and your mom wants her to pay her fair share."

"Oh, my," I groaned. "I'm so sorry. I'll talk to her."

"Don't worry about it," the nurse replied. "I already took care of it."

"Really?" I was almost afraid to ask. "What did you do?"

"I just wrote your mom an I.O.U. and signed Naomi's name to it. They're both fine now."

Another catastrophe averted by a nurse who understood that you cannot argue with someone who has dementia, but you can often easily diffuse a situation by diverting the subject. Mom, fortunately for us (and for Naomi), responded well to diversionary tactics.

Chapter 27

. . . .

IT'S THE RIGHT
THING TO DO

January 12, 2010—

   Meaningless drivel, that's how I characterize many of the conversations that take place around the dining room tables at Grace. I sit with Mom talking with her about nothing. It's not that we don't discuss the news—she finally figured out the other day that America elected a black man as president. We often talk about sports too. She's still a Pittsburgh Steelers fan, and she likes the Orlando Magic basketball team because she vaguely remembers attending Magic games with family members. But most of our conversations revolve around issues at Grace, the food, Mom's latest shower, and of course, the other residents. I tell her my schedule and what the kids are doing, and she always enjoys hearing about them, but I'm not sure she even remembers about whom I am speaking unless I show her a picture, and say, "You remember Kellee, don't you?"

"Oh, yes, of course I do," I know she will answer. "How could I ever forget Kellee?"

But she did.

Sitting with Mom, I sip another cup of coffee from another Styrofoam cup. She likes hers in the gray plastic cups, but I prefer the Styrofoam. It keeps the coffee warmer longer, and frankly the white Styrofoam cups look cleaner to me. While we are toying with our coffee that neither one of us really cares to drink, I overhear one of the family members of another resident sitting at the table behind me. A handsome fellow I guessed to be in his early fifties is telling his mother about the new airport security measures in place after the 2009 Christmas day bombing attempt. She smiles at him weakly, her head nearly resting on her chest. She's barely cognizant of his being there, much less concerned about international air travel. But he's trying desperately to communicate with his mother, to tell her something interesting about his life, and perhaps her former life, with which she can connect. I recognize his frustrations. Meaningless drivel. One-way conversations that at first blush seem as though they are a colossal waste of time. But the conversations may matter more than I can imagine; they keep Mom connected to this world, to her family, to any meaning at all she can find in her daily existence.

During one of her college breaks, my daughter Alyssa asked, "Dad, how can you do this every day? We all love Grandma Minnie, but it is so depressing going to the nursing home. How can you keep doing this?"

I remembered asking my own father a similar question thirty years earlier. When I was a young man, I often went with my father to visit my Aunt Anna, his sister, who suffered from dementia and lived her latter years in a nursing home. The nursing home was about thirty minutes away, so the trip there and back took nearly an hour and if we spent an hour visiting with Aunt Anna, the routine took a chunk of time out of the workday. It was not a fun experience, yet my dad went to see her, day after day, month after month, year after year. The visits were much the same, especially after Aunt Anna lost the ability to communicate verbally. She still smiled at us and laughed for no apparent reason.

When I asked my dad, "How can you do this every day?" he looked at me as though I was speaking a foreign language.

I wasn't being disrespectful; I honestly wanted to know how my dad could maintain such a depressing regimen.

"Why bother?" I asked. "Take a few days off. Aunt Anna won't know if you miss a few days here and there."

"No, but I'll know," my dad responded.

Now it was my turn. I told Alyssa much the same thing as my dad had told me. "We don't visit Grandma Minnie because it is convenient. We come because she loved us before we were even born, and now it is our turn to express unconditional love back to her. We don't come because it is the easy or fun thing to do; we come because it is the right thing to do."

Because Mom had so easily descended our home's carpeted basement steps at Christmas time, when I transferred her from Grace to our house for Easter, I boldly decided to have Mom walk up the basement stairs. My logic was impeccable: Wearing her tennis shoes, she could get better traction on the carpet, plus there were fewer steps than our front porch, and she had a strong banister to which she could cling while making the climb. Easy, right?

Wrong. After struggling up four or five steps, she was exhausted and so was I. As we usually did when ascending steps, I stood beside her, one arm around her waist, and the other hand holding tightly on to hers. But this time, our best efforts weren't working. She stopped halfway and said, "I can't make it."

"Yes, you can, Mom. You have to; I can't carry you up the stairs." I tried standing below Mom on the staircase, holding her with one hand, and putting my shoulder below her rump and pushing. But that made her even more unstable, and for a frightening moment, I thought we both were going to tumble backward down the stairs.

Finally I called out to Lisa. As soon as Lisa came to the top of the stairwell, she recognized that we were in big trouble. She bounded down the stairs and placed her hands under the strong suitcase belt that I had wrapped around Mom's waist before attempting to move her on my own. I'd seen the techs at the rehab control Mom's movement using the belt around her waist to give them a place to grab quickly if she began to fall. I figured I could do the same. What I hadn't figured on was the "dead weight" effect of Mom not being able to move one way or the other, up or down the stairwell. We were stuck.

With Lisa's help pulling her forward, and Mom hanging on to the railing, I pushed, pulled, and cajoled her up the stairway. It took us about twenty minutes to traverse the twenty stairs, and when we got to the top, Mom couldn't go another inch. While I held Mom to keep her from slipping to the floor, Lisa ran and got a chair, sliding it under Mom, allowing her to slump into the chair right in front of the basement doorway. We got her some water and allowed her to rest there for a few minutes before trying to move her any farther.

I was beginning to wonder if this idea of bringing Mom home for the holidays was insane. This Easter would be our last together in our home, of that I was certain. A hollow ache pierced my heart and mind, knowing how much Mom loved to celebrate the resurrection of her Lord Jesus Christ. She loved playing the Easter hymns such as "He Lives!" and "Up From the Grave He Arose,"

"In the Garden," and others. I had set up a portable keyboard for Mom to play, and we placed it near a table so she could play and be a part of the conversations. She enjoyed playing and singing some of those hymns with me before the crowd of visitors arrived.

Mom urinated all over herself several times during Easter dinner. Few smells are more rancid than that of adult urine, and, besides soaking herself, somehow Mom managed to miss the commode and splatter urine all over our bathroom located just off the kitchen. The smell was horrible. Lisa cleaned the mess on her hands and knees, but the smell defied her best efforts. Air fresheners and scented candles proved insufficient to overcome the odor. Only time and more cleaning helped.

Later that afternoon our neighbors Lee and Kim Greenwood stopped by to wish everyone a Happy Easter. Mom no longer recognized the Greenwoods. While we tried to carry on a conversation, she interrupted several times, "Ken, I'm ready to go home."

"Okay, Mom. Just a few minutes," I replied. "We're talking right now."

"I'm tired, and I want to go home," Mom repeated. It was useless to attempt further conversation, so I apologized to our guests and helped Mom down the stairs—the front stairs this time—to my car. She seemed exhausted. When we got back to Grace, I retrieved a wheelchair and transported Mom to her room, where the techs helped her out of her clothes and into bed. It was not yet 5:00 p.m., but she was down for the night.

"Thank you, Ken," she said plaintively, as I prepared to pray with her before leaving. "I'm sorry to bother you, but I'm so glad to be home."

On Saturday evenings when I visited Mom, I frequently asked her to pray for me, since I taught a Sunday school class of about two hundred people. In the spring of 2010, I was teaching Revelation, a book that promises a blessing to all who read and heed its words, but it was not an easy teaching assignment. Sitting side by side on Mom's bed, with Mom dressed in her cotton nightgown ready to be tucked in, I began reading aloud a passage describing Christ's Second Coming. Mom listened carefully as I read. When I finished, she looked at me with tears in her eyes and said, "Won't that be something, when we see Jesus?" Her hand shook slightly as she raised it in front of her. She seemed to be looking off into the future.

My words caught in my throat, but I managed to say, "It sure will be, Mom. What a day that will be."

Almost as if on cue, she began singing the old gospel song, "What a day that will be, when my Jesus I shall see . . ."

I joined in, singing softly along with her, and Mom's voice slipped instinctively into the alto part, harmonizing with me as we sang, "When I look upon His face, the one who saved me by His grace . . ." We sang the entire song, and Mom never missed a word or a note. What a day, what a glorious day that will be.

Chapter 28

THE CHILD WITHIN

I n May 2010 Mom and I established a new routine. Each evening I wheeled her to the front door of the nursing home so
she could wave at me through the window as I pulled out of the
parking area. I steered the car as close as I could get to the door
and rolled down the window so I could wave at her, and she'd sit
in her wheelchair, squeezing her fingers and palm together, in and
out, waving like a toddler might, her face smiling broadly. She'd
lean forward in her wheelchair, straining to see me. She continued
waving until I pulled the car away.

On more than a few occasions, as I departed from Grace with
Mom's face pressed against that window, my eyes clouded. Tears
trickled down my face as I drove off. I reminded myself that she
was in a good place, safe and well cared for.

At such times I prayed, "Why God? Why is she still here?" I
wasn't in a hurry to see her go, but she was ready for heaven. She and
I often talked about the day the clouds would roll away and we'd

see Jesus. She wasn't afraid to die. She was, however, bored at Grace, and felt useless. I took her a book manuscript to proofread as she had so many times before. I thought perhaps seeing the book might trigger memories of working. It didn't. Instead, a pervading sense of uselessness overtook her.

"I just don't know what I'm supposed to be doing here," Mom told me over and over. "I want out of this place."

"But it's nice here, Mom."

"Yes, it is nice. But why am I here? What am I supposed to do?" Tough questions for which I had few answers.

"You're supposed to love people, and tell them about Jesus," I'd encourage her. She'd smile and nod in affirmation. Even with the dementia, she maintained a concern for other people.

On Mother's Day weekend Lisa and I took Mom out to an old-fashioned, "southern cookin'" restaurant.

"I'm not hungry," Mom said as we helped her inside. "My belly is so full!"

"That's okay," I replied. "You can come along with us anyhow, because I'm hungry." I knew that Mom probably didn't remember whether she had eaten or not, and besides, once we sat down, her hunger returned in a flash.

We ordered southern fried chicken, mashed potatoes, green beans, and carrots, and for dessert we enjoyed coconut cream pie, piled high with meringue, much the way Mom used to make it herself. She ate every morsel. Not bad for being full.

As much as I tried to bring freshness to our conversations, they became increasingly stale and repetitive. But around Mother's Day, our daughter and son-in-law gave us something new to talk about. "Mom, guess what? Megan and Keith are going to have a baby."

"Oooh, that's wonderful!" Mom responded. Mom's eyes lit up every time we talked about the baby growing in Megan's belly. But our joy turned to disappointment when Lisa and I showed Mom pictures of pregnant Megan and her husband, Keith, and Mom didn't recognize them.

Nevertheless, I'd remind her frequently about the soon-to-be-born baby, and Mom got as excited as if it were the first time she'd heard the news. It was bittersweet to watch Mom's euphoric response each time I shared with her that Megan and Keith were going to have a baby. I was happy to provide her with moments of joy, but saddened by the obvious truth that she had no recollection of us talking about that same information a few days previously.

Grace had added an enclosed patio to the facility, complete with rocking chairs, picnic tables, and a covered area with plenty of outdoor patio furniture for guests, so I took Mom outside to sit in the sunshine at every opportunity. I had to be careful that she didn't get too much sun, since her skin was now pale and dry. Nevertheless Mom loved sitting outside.

She was convinced that John and Tink and I had built the patio for her, as an addition onto her house. It was futile trying to correct her, so I simply took credit for the patio, passing along kudos to my brothers for their fine work. Mom was particularly concerned about leaving the patio furniture outside at night, especially the red-and-black chair pads. "It might rain," she observed, "or someone might sneak in and steal the pads."

She also took ownership of the tomato plant that somebody was growing in a planter on the patio. Each day I maneuvered her wheelchair over to the plant so she could observe its progress. She got excited when she noticed tiny yellow flower buds on the green branches. Mom recognized that those buds would soon turn into tomatoes. She counted the tomatoes and buds each time we went outside.

It was always good to get Mom outside whenever possible, to get some fresh air and sunshine, but most importantly, for a change of scenery. While too much change can be stressful for someone with dementia, staying inside in the nursing home hallway could be so depressing. My heart always broke when I arrived late in the afternoon and found Mom just sitting in a wheelchair, watching people go by in the hallway. It was hard to believe that two years earlier she was walking and enjoying her life. I guess I knew her becoming a "hallway person" was a possibility, but I had hoped it wouldn't happen so soon.

Although maintaining a familiar routine becomes increasingly important as dementia takes its toll on a person, and diverting from the norm can sometimes cause adverse reactions, Mom still enjoyed getting away from Grace and going out with us whenever possible. A favorite spot was a Chick-fil-A restaurant a few miles away. Although she enjoyed the chicken sandwiches and ice cream, she especially appreciated that the restaurant was not open on Sundays. Not even dementia diminished Mom's reverence for the Sabbath.

The local restaurant employed a large figure dressed like the Chick-fil-A "Eat More Chicken" cow, who danced and played with the children, and Mom loved it. Any time I mentioned Chick-fil-A, Mom replied, "The place with the cow." For some reason, that dancing cow had made an impression on Mom. Even when her memory was nearly gone, whenever I brought up the cow, she'd smile and her eyes would twinkle like a child anticipating the ice cream truck coming through the neighborhood.

Megan and Keith's baby, Stella Pearl, was born on October 3, 2010, just a few days before Mom's eighty-eighth birthday. I took pictures of Stella for Mom to see. "Mom, you are a great-grandmother!" I informed her.

"I know!" Mom replied without hesitation.

"No, Mom. I mean your grandchild Megan just had a baby, so now you are a great-grandmother."

Mom still didn't catch it. "Yes, I know!" she repeated. But she was thrilled to see the pictures of Stella nonetheless. "I better not hold the baby yet," she told me.

"No, we'll go over to Megan and Keith's in a week or two so you can see the baby," I told her. "It probably wouldn't be a good idea to bring the baby here, because there are some sick people here."

"Sick people? Here?" Mom asked.

I nodded.

"You're telling me!" Mom agreed.

Megan, Lisa, and I took Stella Pearl to Grace for the residents' Thanksgiving celebration, a full-blown turkey dinner, albeit with most of the food mashed as soft as possible. Mom was having a bad day and didn't want to get out of bed, but when we placed Stella in her arms, she perked right up. Her eyes brightened and her face broke into a perpetual, adoring smile. She loved holding seven-week-old baby Stella.

We went to the activities room that was decked out in fall harvest festival themes and pilgrims' reminders. Grace provided a lovely meal, but Mom wasn't interested in eating. She held Stella and nestled the baby in her arms the entire meal. I finally figured a way to get Mom to eat. "Megan has to feed the baby, Mom, so you go ahead and eat," I tricked her. Mom smiled and reluctantly allowed Megan to take Stella from her.

Seeing Mom respond so positively to the newest member of our family was tremendously encouraging. She had a lot of love yet to give.

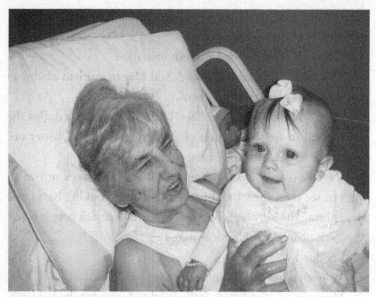

"You're a great-grandmother, Mom."
"I know!"

November 30, 2010—

Recently Mom started calling me "Dad" in conversations. She used to refer to my father as "Dad"; as in, "Hey, Daddy, where have you been?"

Now she frequently confuses me with my dad. "Come sit on the bed here, Dad," she'll say.

I don't bother to correct her.

Chapter 29

STEP DOWN

The day after Thanksgiving we received a call from Grace that they were taking Mom to the hospital to receive antibiotics through an intravenous line. Apparently Mom's foot had been hurting and had turned colors, so one of the nurses feared it might be infected. Everything about the situation sounded so routine I could never have guessed the nightmare Mom was about to endure.

Earlier that week she was complaining about her foot, but Mom often spoke of real or imagined aches and pains, so I didn't pay much attention when she came up with another one. Plus, I knew she had a metal plate in her ankle, and in cold or rainy weather, that often flared on her. Still, I mentioned Mom's discomfort to several nurses at Grace.

"We'll have Dr. D'Amico take a look at it on Tuesday when he's in," Nurse Judy assured me.

By Tuesday Mom's little toe on her right foot was turning red. On Thursday I picked up Mom and transported her to our home for Thanksgiving. She trudged up the front stairs of the house with difficulty, even with assistance from my son-in-law, Keith, and me. She then sat for dinner, but when it came time to go back down the stairs, she balked. "I can't do it, Ken." She was clearly in pain.

Three fellows who were at our home for Thanksgiving and I put Mom on a chair, hoisted her up, and carried her down the front steps to the car. She thanked each of the guys over and over. "I just couldn't make it down those steps tonight," she said. "My foot is really bothering me."

I assumed she was exaggerating, but on Friday Mom's toe turned a dark purple. That's when the nurses at Grace sent her to the hospital for the IV. By the time the ambulance arrived and got her to the emergency room, the toe was black. Gangrene had set in and was ravaging the toe, threatening her entire foot.

Lisa met Mom in the emergency room and was the first to see the toe. The ER doc said, "We need to run some tests and admit her right away to make sure the gangrene isn't in her bloodstream. This does not look good."

When I arrived at the hospital and saw my mom's foot, I was appalled. Mom's toe looked like a cigar that had already been smoked, black and charred and grotesquely foul smelling. The entire room reeked of the rancid gangrene.

"How does something like this happen? And why didn't anyone notice before this?" I had lots of questions, but received few answers.

While Mom was sedated on Friday evening, I talked with her doctors, one a circulation specialist, one a podiatrist/surgeon, and the third, Dr. D'Amico. The circulation guy was a fast-talking young surgeon who tended toward the negative.

"We may be able to save her leg," he told me. "Maybe not. Depends what we find when we get in there and take a look at her veins and arteries. Right now, it doesn't appear that she is getting any blood down to the toes. One toe is already gone; it's dead. It has to come off. The others may need to go, as well." The doctor continued his dire diagnosis. "If it doesn't look as though the foot is healthy, we may as well go ahead and remove the leg from the knee down and fit her with a prosthesis."

"Wait a minute," I wanted to shout. "This is my mom you are talking about. Not some piece of meat that you want to chop up in a bunch of pieces." I wasn't even considering the removal of her leg at that point.

I held my tongue, and rather than protest, I said, "Doctor, would you mind telling these things to Dr. D'Amico, my mom's geriatric doctor? He's been working closely with her over the past year and he can give you a better understanding of what she might be able to overcome physically."

"Certainly," the doctor replied. "I know Dr. D well and we've worked together on a number of patients."

The second doctor had a much better bedside manner. He explained the problem to me. Mom's circulation was so poor that he could barely find a pulse in her ankle, and there were probably plugged arteries or veins that were not allowing the blood to get down to her foot. The toe was already a goner, but hopefully, if the circulation doctor could do an angioplasty and blow out any crud with his magic balloons in her arteries, Mom might still be able to have a foot. If not, well, we'd have to make some tough decisions.

Dr. D'Amico was encouraging and told me that the two surgeons were both highly skilled. They would not do more than necessary, but would not do less, either—assuming I granted permission for the operation.

Since I possessed power of attorney, I had to sign my consent for the surgeon to remove Mom's toe. I felt much like I had when I took my daughters to be vaccinated. They looked at me with such love and trust, and then I took them into the doctor's office where he stabbed them with a needle. Rotten dad. Of course it was for their own good, and signing the papers for the surgeon to whack off my mom's toe was for her own good, too. But I hated signing the paper.

Early Saturday morning Mom was in her hospital room when I arrived. She had no idea that she was about to encounter the first of three operations. She still didn't know what was wrong. "I think I broke my toe," she told me, when I asked her what she'd done and how she might have hurt herself.

I waited in the hospital room with Mom until the orderlies took her downstairs to begin her surgery. "I'll be here when you get back," I told her. I felt like a traitor. They were taking her to cut off her toe, and I didn't want her heart to pound with fear, so I didn't tell her. Or maybe I was the one who was afraid, not Mom.

The surgeon had told me the night before that the procedure would take several hours, so while I waited for Mom to return, I went to the coffee shop. When my cell phone rang, I was surprised to see the doctor's number.

"Ken, we're inside your mom's foot," he said, "and the second toe looks to be infected as well. We can take a chance that after the dead toe is removed, the one next to it may come back, but it doesn't look good. If we don't deal with it now, we may have to bring her back in a few days to remove the second toe. At her age, that could be risky. I'm of the opinion that we should probably remove the second toe now, and give the foot a chance to survive, but I wanted to inform you first."

With great reluctance, I granted the doctor permission to remove not one of my mother's toes, but two. Things were getting ugly.

A few hours later Mom was in the hospital's recovery room, which was a large, open area, with patients in clear view of each other. A dozen or more patients might be in the recovery room at any given time, all hooked up to monitors and IVs. When Mom came out of the recovery room, she was surprisingly lucid. I was afraid that putting her under anesthesia would create more problems for her, but she snapped back quickly. She didn't seem to be aware of what had happened, so I asked her, "How did it go down there?"

"Oh, fine," she responded. "I was just praying for all those sick people in the room."

I gently peeled back the sheet from Mom's feet, holding it up and blocking her view so I could see the surgery area but she could not. When I saw Mom's foot, I wanted to cry. It was bandaged and still oozing blood, but it was clear that two toes were missing from her right foot. I thought immediately of her playing the piano a few months ago, using those toes to press the pedals. I knew she could learn to function with three toes, but I disdained her having to do so.

A second surgery was scheduled two days later, an angioplasty to see if the docs could clean out an artery and get blood down to her foot. They started at the top of her thigh and worked all the way down, getting good blood flow. But when they got to the foot area, everything but one artery was clogged. The surgeon said he couldn't even find a way to bypass the artery, because there was nothing healthy to connect to once he did.

The surgeons used the balloon-type angioplasty to clean out Mom's arteries as best they could, and now there was not much we could do but hope that the blood flow through the one artery was enough to save her remaining toes.

It wasn't.

Within two more days, the doctors said the third toe and a wedgelike section of her foot needed to be removed. Once again she would go under anesthesia, never a totally safe procedure, but especially nerve-racking for someone eighty-eight years of age, who had dementia and was on Coumadin.

This time when the orderlies came to take Mom to surgery, because of her dementia, they asked me to go along with them to answer any questions they might have while they did the prep work. I was glad to go and stayed with her for nearly an hour in the cool recovery room that was doubling as the prep room because the hospital was so busy. Finally the nurses came and told us it was time to go. I prayed with her before leaving.

"I love you, Mom," I said as I squeezed her ice-cold hand. "I'll see you upstairs in a little while."

"Okay," she mumbled. "Be sure you get something to eat."

The operation seemed to be successful, so the next day, while Mom was still recuperating in the hospital, Lisa and I risked being away long enough to attend the college graduation of our middle daughter, Ashleigh, who was graduating a semester early so she could participate as a teacher in an "English as a Second Language" program in Egypt. After the ceremony, Ashleigh, wearing her cap and gown, accompanied me to visit Grandma Minnie in the hospital. Mom had been morose and lethargic, eating very little, and moving with great difficulty, but she broke into a big smile the moment she saw Ashleigh. She was thrilled to know that her granddaughter had graduated.

"What are you going to do now?" Mom asked.

"I'm planning to go to Egypt to teach English to young children," Ashleigh responded.

"Egypt?" Mom asked aghast. "Why Egypt?"

"Well, you know, it is close to Syria," Ashleigh replied. "And that's our ethnic background."

"Oh, well, then, that's okay," Mom said.

Chapter 30

RETURN TO GRACE

After ten days in the hospital, barely eating at all, Mom was discharged, with strict orders that her foot be cleaned and bandaged every day to avoid infection. The nurses and staff at Grace welcomed Mom home, and she responded well to their personal interaction. Her foot looked pathetic, but her spirits rose once she was back among familiar faces.

In January, little more than a month after her surgery, Mom was being transferred from her bed to her wheelchair when she stepped on the big toe of her right foot—the same one from which the doctors had already amputated three toes and a large wedge-of-cheese-like section of her foot. Mom tore the toenail completely off the toe, taking some of the skin with it. Because of the blood thinners, she started bleeding profusely. The nurses were called and they treated the wound, but it was another step down for Mom.

By the time I got there, her foot was bandaged and she was sitting in the dining room at a table all by herself. Her tray of food was in front of her, but she had not eaten. I urged her to eat, but she rebuffed my every attempt.

That same morning I had bumped into Dr. D'Amico at the post office. We talked briefly about my mom's toe, and her debilitating condition. He said he wanted to move her to "Comfort Care," a plan by which the nursing home would not send her to the hospital for every little thing, but would rather treat her right there at Grace. That didn't seem much different to me from what we were already doing, but I told him I would consider it. Then the doctor told me, "Your mom is not doing well. I'm concerned that she is not eating. I think we're looking at about six months."

His words stunned me at first, but I knew immediately what he was talking about, and perhaps what surprised me most was my own acquiescence to his prognosis. I nodded and said, "Yes, I understand."

Sadness swept over me. Of course, I knew from the day Mom entered Grace that she'd probably die there. We all understood that. She wasn't going to get better; it was simply a matter of taking the best care of her that we could during her final years. Keep her comfortable, safe, well fed, with nursing care as needed. That was the plan. But now the doctor was predicting her demise.

Six months? Did I understand? Really? Did I understand that he was talking about Mom dying? I didn't want to accept it.

Later that same day while visiting Mom, I pushed her wheelchair over to the piano so she could play. "Don't try to use the pedals," I warned her, making sure the wheelchair was just far enough away that she couldn't reach the pedals. The last thing she needed was to break open the skin on her healing foot.

At first she didn't want to play. "I'm too tired," she said in barely a whisper. "I can't remember."

"Yes, you can, Mom," I encouraged her. "Let's just try one or two songs. I'll sing; you play."

I sang a few lines of "Amazing Grace"; she didn't move. That was a first. She had always played along, even if she didn't sing. I placed my hands on the keyboard, and although I'm not a piano player, I knew a few chords, enough to play the chorus of a song she loved: "To Be Like Jesus." I played one finger at a time as I sang along with my bare-bones melody. After a few measures, I heard her softly singing harmony with me. "To be like Jesus, to be like Jesus . . . All through life's trials, from earth to heaven, all I ask is to be like Him."

I flipped through the pages of a hymnbook sitting on the piano. She had great difficulty remembering the old hymns that she ordinarily could play without even looking at the music. I found some of Mom's favorites: "I Love to Tell the Story" and "The Old Rugged Cross," and then I found a song titled, "When I've Gone the Last Mile of the Way." I put the hymnbook on the piano and pointed to the music.

Once, when she was lucid, Mom had told me that she wanted to have this song sung at her funeral.

January 17, 2011—

"I didn't get to go to Dad's grave site today," Mom told me sadly. She hasn't been to his grave site in more than ten years.

She spoke a great deal about her brother Jim, and expressed how worried she was about his eternal salvation. She had cared for Uncle Jim when he was sick, prior to having to put him into a nursing home. Mom hated having to rely on other people to care for him. She felt it was her responsibility. And she did it for as long as possible. Now it's my turn to emulate her role.

In mid-January Mom had a follow-up appointment with her surgeons. The doctor unwrapped Mom's foot and began scraping the skin so it would bleed. "The health is in the blood," she said, looking up at me. Mom did well until the surgeon began cutting away dead skin around the area of her foot where the bone was totally exposed. "Oh, Doctor, please," she cried out.

"Hold my hand, Mom," I said, "and squeeze as tight as you can." She tried but her strength was weak and the doctor's scalpel was sharp.

"What do you think about those Steelers?" the surgeon asked, knowing my mom hailed from the Pittsburgh area. "How about that Polamalu?"

"He's great, isn't he, Mom?" I squeezed her hand as I spoke. "Hey, do you remember when I had long, bushy hair like that?"

The surgeon was literally sitting on the floor, cutting dead skin away from the open wound area. "Oh," Mom gasped. But then, rather than crying out in pain, she said, "Oh, Ken, please don't make me laugh!"

I burst out laughing, Mom did, too, and we all relaxed. "Okay, Mom. I'll be quiet." The doctor continued ridding Mom's foot of the dead tissue so the healthy pink skin could grow. By the time she finished and bandaged the foot again, Mom had almost fallen asleep in the chair. The doctor and I entered that weird dementia twilight zone, the state of talking about the patient as though she wasn't in the room.

"How long do you think it will take for this to heal?" I asked, nodding at what looked like a bloody piece of meat in a butcher's shop; the mess that was once my mom's foot.

"With her low blood flow, and her not eating enough to provide nutrition to the wound area, it could possibly take as much as a year," the surgeon replied.

"A year?" My mind went to my recent conversation with Dr. D'Amico in which he said he didn't think Mom had much more than six months to live.

"You may want to consider us taking off more of the leg, amputating up to the knee," the doctor suggested. "That's where her leg has three arteries bringing blood."

Despite the doctors' dire predictions, by springtime Mom's spirits brightened, and she remained upbeat and positive.

"Hi, Miss Minnie. How are you today?" a nurse or staff member might ask.

"Never better!" she'd respond.

Never better. With her total existence confined to a bed or a wheelchair, with three of her toes and a third of her foot amputated, her memory gone, and her body betraying her at every level, Mom had the audacity to declare that she was "never better."

That's faith.

Chapter 31

I CAN'T FIND MY TOES

M om often sat out in the hallway watching the nurses and visitors going by. When she saw me coming down the hall, her face lifted and she smiled. "Hey! Where have you been?"

"Oh, just working. How are you feeling?" I ask.

"I feel good," Mom said emphatically. "And I look good too!"

In April we were out on the patio, Mom sitting in her wheelchair and me sitting on the picnic table bench, enjoying the spring sunshine when Mom noticed something unusual about her right foot. "I can't find my toes," she said plaintively.

This was the first direct statement that indicated she had any awareness that three of her toes and a third or more of her foot were missing. I wasn't sure how to respond, so as I often did with Mom, I tried the lighthearted approach. "Oh, don't worry, Mom. We'll find them a little later."

She looked up at me, then back down at her wedge-shaped

foot with two toes sticking out from beneath the bandages. "Yeah, they're probably around here somewhere," she said.

Later that day I received a call from Grace requesting permission to have Mom sleep in a different room that night. Naomi, her roommate since the day she had arrived at Grace, was not doing well, and most likely would not survive the night. The social worker thought it might be easier on both my mom and Naomi's family if Mom were not there when Naomi passed away. I agreed.

That night Mom slept in a room down the hall, and early the next morning Naomi slipped into eternity. I didn't know how to tell Mom, or even if I should. I knew she loved Naomi, and that she watched out for her, yet the reality was that if I didn't say a word about Naomi, Mom might not even realize she was gone. Her friendship with Naomi resided in the short-term memory bank.

I decided to wait a day or two and see if Mom noticed that Naomi was missing.

She never mentioned her again.

Oddly enough, Mom did remember Amy Grant. Amy's mom, Gloria Grant, passed away a few days after Easter that year. She was eighty years of age and had suffered dementia the final few years of her life. At the funeral, Amy shared a poignant story that resonated with me. At the conclusion of a visit with her mom at her bedside, Amy said, "I have to go now, Mom. I'm singing a concert tonight."

Amy's mom looked at her and asked, "Oh, Amy, do you sing?"

"Yes, Mom. I sing a little."

"Oh, good," her mother responded. "Amy, sing about what matters."

When I told Mom that Amy's mother had passed away, she was deeply moved. "Oh, that's too bad. Please tell Amy I'm sorry." Then, almost as an afterthought, while still sitting in her wheelchair, Mom said, "I need to go out and get her a sympathy card."

Like all recent holidays, Mothers Day 2011 was difficult. Mom's hair was combed and teased neatly, and she was dressed in an attractive outfit as she sat slumped over in her wheelchair in the hallway. She didn't notice that I had come in until I kissed her on the cheek. We sat outside on the patio, and I called my brothers so they could wish her a happy Mother's Day and reminisce about past celebrations. I grieved that, in many ways, our mom was gone, and I missed her.

The next day it was 88 degrees so I took Mom outside to get some sunshine. The serotonin was good for her. We sat for a while in the patio area, but it got too warm, so I pushed her around the building to allow her to enjoy the parklike setting. At one point she could tell that I was exerting some effort to push the wheelchair up a slight grade in the road. She turned in her chair, looked back at me, and asked, "Do you want me to push you?"

"Naw, that's okay, Mom. You used to push me in a stroller a long time ago. Now it's my turn to push you."

"Oh, okay. But if you want me to push you, just let me know."

"Okay, Mom. I will."

Around Memorial Day John came to visit Mom. He hadn't seen her since before the gangrene incident and he was visibly shaken at her appearance. Not to mention that she couldn't remember his name. She seemed to recognize his face, but kneeling over her bed—which had been lowered to about twelve inches off the floor in case she happened to roll out—he had to remind her that he was her oldest son. Eventually, when Mom figured out that it was John, not just me, she was seeing, her features brightened. The second day of his visit, when we came in we found Mom sitting slumped over, her right arm hanging down the side of the wheelchair, her head cocked to one side. For a moment we weren't sure whether she was dead or alive. We awakened her, and propped pillows under her side to straighten her, but she still had difficulty sitting upright.

As he usually did, John stayed for several days visiting Mom. They were long, uneventful hours sitting by her side, with Mom less communicative than ever. The day he was leaving, I went to get the car so he could have some time alone with Mom. As he said goodbye to her, he became deeply emotional, his face turned red, and his eyes filled with tears. We all knew each good-bye could be the last.

In late May I attended another seminar conducted by Dr. D'Amico on the subjects of Alzheimer's and dementia. As always, the doctor's presentation was informative, yet offered no real solutions. Afterward he and I talked briefly about my mom's debilitating condition and he made a statement that stunned me.

"Your mom will die from something and the medical profession will put a name on it—pneumonia, or something else—but the real cause will be dementia. Her body can no longer function properly because her brain is not functioning properly."

The doctor's track record for being right on target with his calls regarding Mom made his statement all the more profound to me. Prior to this I had always regarded dementia as a rather innocuous nuisance, slowly robbing my mom of her mental acuity, but not malicious in nature. Now I saw dementia differently. No matter what the cause of death, excluding something highly unusual such as a natural disaster or death because of a fall, Mom's eventual demise would not be caused by ill health, heart problems, or other usual sources. Dementia would kill her.

May 27, 2011—

Mom is talking a lot of gibberish these days, sometimes using real words, sometimes not. But the sentences don't connect. She tells me that she has been outside to the store, or driving the car, which of course she has not.

❧

Mom was in bed sleeping when I arrived one afternoon around 2:30. The shades were pulled down and the lights were out. She was fully dressed, but under her covers.

I roused her from her sleep and raised her hospital-style bed so she could sit up in it. "There's just not much to do here," she said.

"Well, did you play bingo today?" I asked.

"I did," she answered. "I told them, 'I don't know how to play,' and they said, 'Come on, anyhow. It's fun.' So I played. And you know what? It is fun."

"Yep, it is, Mom," I replied, knowing that she had just played bingo the previous week. She had formerly loved to play bingo, and the social director made sure that Mom always won something, a stuffed animal, a special ribbon, or a picture. Now Mom could barely remember how to play. She still won prizes, but we were losing the game.

Chapter 32

. . . .

WHY MUST SHE GO THROUGH THIS?

It wasn't the alarm clock that awakened me around 6:00 a.m. on Sunday morning, June 5, but a phone call from a nurse at Grace. "Your mom's breathing is erratic, she was shaking like a leaf and fevered, and her oxygen levels were down. She seems to be breathing better now that we put her on oxygen, but she is still a bit blue."

"What do you suggest?" I asked.

"Well, if she were my mother, I'd want her in the hospital."

"Okay, let's do that."

Mom was sent by ambulance to the hospital ER, where Lisa and I found her lying when we arrived. A sheet covered her chest and stomach, but she was exposed from the waist down. I pulled the hospital sheet down over Mom's legs. She'd have been embarrassed had she known she was so naked to passersby in the ER, even if they were mostly hospital personnel. When I tried to talk with her, Mom could not speak. She made sounds much like a baby might before learning to talk. That was about it. I asked her questions. "Are you hurting anywhere? Did you fall?" She couldn't answer.

"The doctor has already taken some tests and we're awaiting the results," a nurse informed us. "It will probably be about an hour or so before we know anything."

While we waited for the test results, Lisa and I tried to make Mom comfortable. I held her hand at times, and she seemed able to squeeze mine. That was a good sign.

Since there was little we could do other than keep Mom awake, I told her that I'd go teach Sunday school class and I'd be back. "Please pray for me," I said, knowing how effective her prayers were, but also how the duty of praying for me often stimulated her.

Before I left, Lisa and I sang a few hymns to my mom, "What a Friend We Have in Jesus," "Amazing Grace," and "What a Day That Will Be."

By the time I returned, an hour or so later, she had perked up enough to answer questions. She was barely coherent, but at least she spoke in sentences rather than gibberish. The doctor decided to admit her, since she had what he called "a raging urinary infection."

That wasn't so bad. Mom didn't drink enough water, and urinary infections were now part of our regular vocabulary. Totally treatable with antibiotics and liquids, Mom's condition didn't worry me. A few days in the hospital, and hopefully, she'd be okay.

That evening before leaving the hospital, I spoke specifically to the nurses about Mom's medications. "Please don't give her pain meds unless absolutely necessary. They knock her out and she won't eat or drink. She's tough. She went through three major operations six months ago on Tylenol 3 alone, so if we can avoid the stronger medication, she will respond better."

"All right," the nurse on duty said. "I'll note that and be sure to ask her doctor."

When I arrived at the hospital early Monday morning, Mom was knocked out. They'd given her strong pain meds. I was furious, but there was little I could do. I called Dr. D'Amico and asked him to emphasize to the hospital staff that pain medication incapacitated my mom.

Tuesday morning, June 7, with Mom still in the hospital, Lisa and I had to decide whether or not to go on a short family vacation we had planned in conjunction with picking up Alyssa from a college honors program in Florida. I certainly didn't want to leave Mom alone in the hospital, with no family members in town, so I called John, and he agreed to return to Nashville to stay with Mom while we were gone.

Mom seemed to be doing much better, so I felt confident that she would be returning to Grace once the infection subsided. But the bluish-purple color of her remaining two toes on her right foot concerned me. Before leaving I pointed out the spots to one of the male nurses, and he promised to have Mom's circulatory doctor take a look.

Sure enough, when I called for a report on Wednesday, John told me the doctors were worried about more gangrene setting into her toes because of the poor circulation. Midmorning, her circulatory doctor called. He explained his plan to clear Mom's arteries if there was enough blood flow, but if not, he'd have her surgeons on hand to remove the toe or toes that were dying. I felt a sick feeling in my stomach as I drove home. I understood that the surgeons had her best interests in mind, but they were chopping up my mom, one piece at a time.

Once in the operating room, the decision to amputate Mom's fourth toe was unavoidable. It was either that or let the infection ravage her entire body. Mom made it through yet another operation, but once out of recovery, she refused to eat.

Overnight Mom's temperature rose, so the docs unwrapped the foot to check for black skin, which would indicate deadness. Her one remaining toe looked awful, with a dangerous telltale black spot on its tip. Looking at the toe, I knew it was just a few squirts of blood away from turning gangrenous. The doctor poked, probed, and prodded the skin around the surgery. Finally she seemed satisfied. "I'll order an IV drip of antibiotics and get her back to Grace," she said.

Afterward I tried to convince Mom to eat something. She ate a few green beans, a few orange slices, and a bit of ice cream. That's all.

"I'm going to work and I'll be back in a few hours," I told her.

"Okay, you come back and I'll take care of you," she said.

"I love you, Mom. See you later," I called as I waved good-bye and stepped out of her hospital room.

She waved weakly and had the faintest bit of a smile on her face as she said, "I love you, too, son."

I walked to the elevator, asking God for the thousandth time, "Why? Why must she suffer such indignity at this stage in her life?" Watching Mom's daily demise evoked so many questions. Why didn't the Lord just take her home? She has loved Jesus all her life; she has a firm belief in God, and is ready to go. After such a robust life, it was almost a mockery to see her so frail.

The "why" questions pummeled my mind more than I cared to admit. Surely she couldn't still be here suffering so she could learn something. She must be here for our benefit, for me, so I can learn something more of how to live—and how to die, complete in Jesus, regardless how many fingers or toes a person might have.

"Help me to understand the lesson, Lord," I prayed. "Don't let me miss whatever it is I am supposed to learn from all this, at such horrendous expense to Mom." I choked back my tears as I stepped inside the elevator and the doors whisked closed.

Chapter 33

HOMEWARD BOUND

After her twelfth day in the hospital, Mom's doctor was still concerned about a black spot the size of a dime on her big toe. He was also concerned that she could not or would not straighten out her leg. Instead she pulled her knee up into a fetal position. The leg had atrophied severely since the initial surgeries. For the first time, I wondered if we'd made a mistake in not encouraging the doctors to amputate Mom's leg all the way up to her knee after the first bout with circulatory problems.

More disconcerting, the doctors asked my permission to insert a feeding tube down her throat. Images of Terri Schiavo immediately darted across my mind. I redoubled my efforts to feed Mom manually. Try as I might, I could convince her to eat only a few green beans and a few nibbles of pasta.

I put a small amount of melted ice cream on a spoon and placed it to her mouth. She sipped at the ice cream as though she were tasting a nasty cough medicine. But at least I was getting something into her, so I scooped up more ice cream and placed it up to her lips. Most of the ice cream ran down her chin, or slipped out the sides of her mouth, but she sipped in a few drops. I continued the process for about half an hour, until she finally said, "No more."

"One more bite," I said, pressing a quarter teaspoonful of ice cream to her mouth. Mom pursed her lips tightly shut. She had dementia, but she could still be stubborn when she wanted to be. I found a napkin and wiped the vanilla ice cream off her chin.

A tech who tried to feed Mom did little better. She finally gave up in frustration. Later that afternoon, the hospital dietician came in the room.

"I understand we need to arrange a feeding tube for Mrs. Abraham," she said. "She needs to get some nutrition if that foot is going to heal. And since she is not eating at all, this might be the best way for now."

"I don't want her to be on the tube permanently," I said. "She went through a similar food withdrawal last time she was in the hospital. If we can get her home and back into a familiar environment, maybe her appetite will pick up again. That's what happened before."

"I understand," the dietician said with a condescending smile, as though to say, "Don't try to tell me my business, buddy. I do this sort of thing every day."

"My mom is a strong person," I said. "She won't do well with a tube down her throat. She pulled off the oxygen mask when we first came in here last week."

"We have ways of dealing with that," the dietician said. No doubt she didn't mean it as a threat, but her comment sounded ominous.

"Well, let's give it a try," I said, "but if she resists too much, I'll want the tube removed. She's a good, compliant patient. Surely we can get her to eat somehow."

The dietician gave me another condescending look, tapped her clipboard, and said good-bye.

When I checked with Dr. D'Amico, he was both reassuring and characteristically blunt. "We can receive her back to Grace with the feeding tube," he said. "Hopefully, the nutrition through the tube will stimulate her appetite and she can begin eating on her own once again." The doctor paused, as though he knew I wouldn't want to hear what he was about to say. "But if they want to put a tube directly into her stomach, we may need to start thinking about end-of-life care. Many dementia patients simply stop eating at this stage. They just don't want to eat anymore, so they won't. You and I have talked about that before, and I've not pulled any punches with you, so I'm not going to start now. If they put a permanent feeding tube into her stomach, it is simply prolonging her life artificially, and your mom and you expressly said you did not want that."

"I understand, Doctor," I replied quietly. "At this point we're going to try the feeding tube down her throat."

"Let's give her till Monday and see how we're doing," the doctor said.

"Okay. Monday," I repeated. Monday would be Mom's fifteenth day in the hospital without any significant intake of food.

The feeding tube was a spaghetti-like tunnel of plastic in her mouth, running down her throat. Mom didn't handle the tube well—who would? She repeatedly pulled it out. Finally the nurses gave up, and the doctor rescinded the order.

When Lisa and I visited Mom on Saturday evening, she asked, "What's the answer? I want to know the answer."

"What do you want to know?" Lisa asked. "What's the question?"

"When is Jesus coming?" Mom asked clear as a bell.

"I don't know," I responded, "but I don't think it will be long."

"Please, Jesus, please come," Mom said.

"He will, Mom," I assured her.

"Please, Jesus; please come now. I'm tired. I want my legs to stop hurting. I want to go home. Please, Jesus. Please come."

I wanted to tell her, "It's okay, Mom. You can go home. I release you to go. We'll be fine here, and we'll see you again there soon." That's what I was thinking, but I couldn't get the words past the lump in my throat.

I met with the doctor Sunday afternoon outside Mom's hospital room. He insisted on putting a feeding tube into her stomach, and I was nearly ready to acquiesce, but I felt that the artificial feeding was not in Mom's best interests. What a tough decision! Who am I to say whether she should continue to eat through a tube until her body gives up? I racked my brain, called my brothers, and talked with several friends whose spiritual wisdom I regarded highly. I posed the same question to all of them: Was I making the right decision by refusing the feeding tube?

Their answers came back a unanimous "yes."

I asked the doctor to get Mom back to Grace where she could at least be in her own environment. The hospital personnel were good at keeping her clean and turning her on her bed so she didn't develop bedsores, but all the poking and prodding and three intravenous tubes running into her body simply were not helping Mom. Maybe if she was back in her own environment, she might rally. It was worth a try.

That evening Mom seemed slightly more alert, so I tried lifting her spirits by singing to her. I quietly broke into a verse of "Victory in Jesus," and before long, I heard her trying to sing along with me. Her voice was feeble and raspy, but she was able to mouth the words: "O Victory in Jesus, my Savior forever, He sought me and bought me, with His redeeming blood, He loved me ere I knew Him, and all my love is due Him. He plunged me to victory . . . ."

The next day, after Dr. D'Amico contacted the doctor at the hospital, we finally arranged to have Mom returned to Grace. The hospital doctor was quite negative about releasing Mom, wanting to put her on antibiotics for six weeks, but as Dr. D'Amico pointed out in his usual direct manner, "She won't be alive if we leave her in the hospital another six weeks." He was equally blunt in talking with me about Mom's future.

"We're looking at end-of-life care," he said matter-of-factly. "We can do hospice care at Grace."

I didn't understand how that differed a great deal from what we were already doing—maintaining Mom's condition and comfort, without trying to do "extraordinary" procedures to get her well—but I realized the implications.

"Basically, we've done all we can do for her. Her system is shutting down, and she may not turn this around. You need to be prepared for that," he said.

I beat the ambulance to Grace, went inside, and greeted several of the nurses, technicians, and residents. "How's Minnie?" everyone wanted to know. "When is she coming back?"

"She should be here any minute."

"Oh, good!" one of the nurses said.

"I'm so glad," a resident said. "I've missed her smile."

It was truly a homecoming atmosphere when the paramedics wheeled Mom down the hallway on an ambulance gurney. Mom was groggy and extremely weak, so I leaned over the railing as I caught the gait of the paramedics, walked along with them, and said, "Hey, Mom, you're back home. Everybody's been asking about you."

"Home," she repeated. "Am I home?"

"Yes, you are home," I replied, oblivious to how silly that sounded as she returned to her half of an eight-by-ten-foot room. Still, to Mom, "Graceland" was home.

Tommy, one of the male nurses at Grace, and Connie, his assistant, pulled the hospital curtains shut and went to work on Mom as soon as the paramedics lifted her onto her bed. Ruth, her new roommate, called out her greetings. Mom didn't reply.

"She seems a bit sedated," I told Ruth as I stepped out of the way of the nurses and into Ruth's half of the room. "But I think once she wakes up, she'll be more talkative." I didn't want Ruth to think Mom was being rude by not responding. Relationships between nursing home residents can be delicate; I didn't want to needlessly create ill feelings.

Tommy and Connie and another tech, Melanie, weighed my mom in a scale that looked like an old-fashioned potato scale in a general store, with strong Mylar fabric holding Mom in the air. Melanie held Mom's head, but she soon was able to hold it up by herself—a good sign, I thought. Watching the numbers on the scale, I expected them to rise higher. They didn't. Mom weighed a mere 120 pounds. She had weighed 168 when she first entered Grace more than two years earlier; she weighed 140 after the hospitalization in December, and now she was down to less than she weighed on her wedding day. She looked pathetic hanging there above her bed, her drooping skin loose and pale, looking much like a sack of skin that happened to contain her spirit.

Mom's blood pressure was good, better than mine, and her temperature was around 97.3, a far cry from the infection that had wracked her body a few days earlier.

Tommy explained each procedure to me as he and Connie worked on Mom.

"We're checking for any signs of skin damage, any bruises, bedsores, or areas we need to treat," he said. He gently unwrapped Mom's foot, revealing the red, black, and cream-colored areas from the most recent amputation. He carefully applied a new bandage and wrapped Mom's foot again. Connie tried to get Mom to straighten out her right leg, but she couldn't do it.

"We'll have to do some physical therapy and take it slow. It seems like it might hurt her if I try to force the leg down."

I nodded. "As far as I know, she hasn't straightened out that leg since she left here fifteen days ago."

The nurses removed Mom's diaper, raising her hospital gown up to her shoulder as they examined her. With any patient, bedsores are always a possibility during a long hospitalization, but with dementia patients, the potential problems are exacerbated because they don't remember to move. In Mom's case, she seemed unable to move while in the hospital. Sure enough, red areas of skin irritation were evident on her bum. More concerning was an inch-long sore on her buttocks, slit open like an eye that was squinting. The nurses applied medicated salve to the sores and other discolored areas.

Connie succeeded in getting Mom to drink a few sips of a strawberry "Mighty Shake," the nutrient-fortified drink on which Mom was surviving. They worked on Mom for about half an hour, getting her situated, her diaper changed, fresh bandages, and then they finally covered her up and tucked her into bed. Throughout the process, the nurses referred to my mom as "Miss Minnie." She recognized their faces, although she doubtless did not remember any names. Still, she seemed remarkably at peace and content being back at Grace. She was "home."

The nurses finished up, and when we were finally alone, I leaned over Mom's bed, and said, "How about that, Mom? You're tucked into your own bed. Isn't that great?"

She opened her eyes, as if she'd been fully cognizant through-out the entire ordeal, and said, "Thank you, Jesus!"

I laughed. Her condition hadn't improved one iota, but she was happy and content. That was the best we could do for her, and for now, it was enough.

Chapter 34

Now It's Time to Say Good-bye

The next few days were touch and go, with Mom making slight progress, drinking her "Mighty Shakes," and eating a few bites of breakfast. She was horribly weak, but she seemed in good spirits and thrilled to be back among familiar faces at Grace. Reality pinched at my idealism, though, when I met with Brenda, the director of nursing, Kerri, the social director, and Andrea, Grace's admissions director. They were kind but straightforward in describing Mom's condition.

"Your mom has osteomyelitis," Brenda said. "It's an infection in her bones. The usual treatment would be about six weeks of strong antibiotics given intravenously in the hospital. But, as you and Dr. D'Amico have agreed, that would not work well for your mom. Because she is not eating, she would starve to death or develop other complications, and she is too weak for more operations. She also has some serious bedsores, not because the hospital didn't move her, but because her entire system is shutting down. The bone infection is serious, and if those sores turn septic, or if the infection gets into her blood, there's not much we'll be able to do."

We talked about what symptoms Mom might develop and what alternatives we might have for medications. It seemed a foregone conclusion that Mom would not be getting well, apart from a supernatural touch from God. And that didn't seem to be happening. Or maybe it was occurring in a way that I didn't want to accept.

I talked with Tink and encouraged him to bring the kids to see their Grandma while there was still time. "She is fading fast," I told him.

When John had seen her in June, he had said his final good-byes. "Unless you really need me, I don't think I can do this again," he had told me. "The next time I see her," he said, as I returned him to the airport, "will be at her funeral in Pennsylvania."

The techs were good about encouraging Mom to eat, but by Monday, June 21, she hadn't eaten a full meal in nearly a month. I tried feeding her like I might feed our grandbaby, Stella, holding the ice cream to her lips until it either slipped inside her mouth or dripped down her face. Mom wasn't belligerent; she seemed to be trying. But it was like trying to eat ice cream after going to the dentist and having your jaw filled with Novocain. Her mouth simply wouldn't move. Her hair was matted, and when I brushed my hand through it, the usually soft texture of her hair felt more like a Brillo pad.

Before I left Mom on Monday evening, I smoothed her hair, and told her that Tink and his daughter, Kellee, were flying in to see her the next day.

"Oooh, that's wonderful," Mom squealed like a little child. "I'll be so happy to see them." As I did every night before leaving,

I lowered Mom's bed to twelve inches off the floor. When I knelt on the rubber floor pad to pray with her and kiss her good night, Mom could barely lift her head.

Although I didn't tell Mom, I had also encouraged our daughters, Ashleigh and Alyssa, to come home from college that weekend, which they did. I sensed that opportunities to visit with their grandmother while she was semiaware of their presence would be limited.

The following day I picked up the family members at the airport, and Lisa and I escorted them to Grace. On the way, I tried to prepare them for the worst.

"Grandma may not know you," I warned everyone. "It has been quite awhile since she's seen you and her memory is not good these days. Plus, she just came out of the hospital following another traumatic experience."

"No problem," Tink replied. "We'll just roll with it."

We signed in at Grace and headed toward Mom's room. On the way, we passed a woman sitting in a wheelchair, with her head drooping down almost onto her chest. The woman was dressed in what appeared to be Mom's clothing. "I can't believe they get her clothes so confused," Lisa said as we passed by. Lisa worked hard to make sure Mom's clothes were clean and her outfits matched, yet occasionally we'd find her wearing someone else's clothes or another woman wearing something of Mom's.

As we passed by the woman dressed in Mom's clothing, Kellee cried out, "Grandma!"

We wheeled around on our heels. Sure enough, there in the hallway, dressed in one of her nicer outfits, was Mom. Christie, the in-house beautician at Grace, had done Mom's hair, and although she was quite feeble, she looked fantastic! She was a different woman than the person I had left the night before.

Seeing the family members from Florida, as well as Ashleigh and Alyssa, lifted Mom's spirits immeasurably. The next day we took her out onto the patio at Grace, and Kellee put a pair of sunglasses on Mom so the sun wouldn't bother her eyes. Her hands were swollen, as were her legs, and her foot was bleeding, but, in her blue-and-white dress and her shades, she looked like a movie star. Megan, Keith, and Stella came along to visit Grandma Minnie too.

"I'm going home. I just wanted to say good-bye before I leave."

We carefully let Mom hold Stella, who was now nearly nine months old, and adorably cute, but an energetic, squiggly baby. Mom nestled her great-granddaughter close to her chest, and Stella rested, contented and quiet. Although we enjoyed being together, everyone recognized that this would be the last time on earth that we'd be gathered like this.

We called John from the patio, as we'd done a hundred times previously. Today, though, after going through the usual questions about how she was feeling, Mom said to John, "Well, I just wanted to call and say good-bye before I go."

"Where are you going?" my older brother asked.

"I'm going home," Mom replied. "And I wanted to say good-bye before I leave."

It was one of those poignant moments when Mom's words possessed multiple meanings. To us, she was saying good-bye before going home to heaven.

Chapter 35

BRINGING IN REINFORCEMENTS

I met with representatives of a hospice organization to discuss Mom's care. "We don't want to do anything heroic," they told me. "We just want to keep her comfortable until she makes her journey to the other side." It struck me that the hospice workers were reluctant to use the words *death, die,* or *dying.* But we all understood what we were admitting: "Minnie Abraham is going to die any day now, so let's do what we can to make that as simple as possible for her."

I wrestled with the ramifications of signing the hospice orders. Who was I to be making such potentially life-ending decisions? Dying with dignity—I had never really thought much about that previously. In signing, was I tacitly admitting that Mom's life was over, that all we could do now was to keep her comfortable and wait? Was I ruling out that God could perform a miracle? By signing was I saying that it was my choice whether my mother lived or died? Certainly, my brothers and I had power of attorney, and I was within the parameters of my legal responsibilities to make that call, but was it the right decision? Was it the right thing to do before God?

I called my brothers and we talked through the issues. We couldn't ignore the obvious. Mom was dying, and apart from a miracle, she would not recover here on earth. And even if she did, she would have no meaningful existence. Hospice was willing to help her all the way to the end and beyond. We'd be foolish to reject their assistance.

In reviewing the documents, I felt as though I were reading Mom's death warrant, although everyone involved reassured me that I was making the right choice. Still, there was something so final about those documents. The gentleman from hospice reminded me that if Mom rallied, she could return to regular care. He reiterated that we believed in God, that we believed in miracles. Yet I felt as though I was giving up on God's willingness to heal my mom.

Of course I knew that was not the case; her life, like mine, was in God's hands. But now that I was concurring with the doctors' assessment that they had done all they could, I grappled with those thoughts. I signed the papers, acknowledging that unless the Lord had some reason to keep her around, something He wanted us to learn, Mom was on her way home.

The bedsores on Mom's bottom exacerbated her discomfort. "I want to get out of here," she told me.

"I know, Mom," I said, wondering whether she meant getting out of Grace, or getting out of this existence. Instead I focused on getting her out of the wheelchair. "I'll find a nurse who can help get you into bed."

About that time Nurse Pam came along and noticed Mom's toe bleeding. She was on her way out the door and headed home for the day, but she stopped and took time to go back inside and get some antiseptic for the bedsores and bandages for Mom's toe. Many of the staff members at long-term-care facilities don't receive high wages. They don't work for a paycheck; they do it out of love. Pam is one of those kind souls.

We received an early morning phone call from Julie, a hospice nurse, asking permission to order morphine for Mom's pain. I consented, adding, "I don't want her to be in intense pain, but if she can handle it with Tylenol 3, that would be my preference. The heavier drugs knock my mom out."

When I arrived at Grace, Chastity, a tech caring for Mom, was excited. "Your mom ate everything on her plate," Chastity gushed.

"You're kidding!" I replied.

"And she was looking for more."

"Chastity, you must be a miracle worker. That's the most my mom has eaten in over a month!"

Chastity smiled. "Well, I believe in miracles."

"Me too," I said.

It was a short-lived celebration. We discovered that one of the sores on Mom's hip had turned from pink to purple—not good. Pam ordered more medication be applied, but Mom's condition was deteriorating. She was extremely tired, and could hardly stay awake during our visit, but at least she had eaten something.

I spent hours sitting in the chair next to Mom's bed, holding her hand, watching her breathing, a staccato of short breaths along with an occasional longer gasp for air. I noticed that her hands, though colder than normal, had grown unusually soft. Those hands had often been held by many people, clutching on to Mom for dear life, as she had prayed for them and encouraged them to keep trusting in Jesus. "God answers prayer," she'd say, as she held the person's hands. "And prayer changes things." Remembering how those hands once held me, comforted me, disciplined me, expressed love to me, I spoke, although I wasn't sure Mom could hear me.

"God answers prayer, Mom, and you know, prayer changes things." Now her hands were turning colder, tinted by an unearthly color of bluish purple as the blood fought unsuccessfully to circulate throughout her body. I knew it wouldn't be long until her entire body was as cold as those soft hands.

She was in a great deal of pain, saying, "My legs hurt so bad, I just can't take it any more." I tried to reassure her that the medicine was going to kick in at any time and would help her to feel better. "I want to go home," she said, "but I'm not sure where home is, and who is going to move my stuff?"

"Don't worry, Mom. I'm taking care of everything. John and Tink will help too. You'll be fine." I looked at her bandaged feet. "And the Lord is touching your feet and restoring them."

A faint smile creased Mom's face. Soon the Lord would be restoring her entire body, and she seemed to know it.

Increasingly I was running to the phone every time it rang. I didn't dare miss a call. Requests from Grace regarding increases in Mom's medication became more frequent. I recognized that "the call" could come at any moment.

Keeping the family informed about Mom's condition dominated most of the phone conversations I initiated. I didn't expect the family in Florida to do anything, but I wanted them to understand that we were getting close to Mom's departure.

Checking on funeral details while Mom was still alive seemed especially morbid, but since our family had decided that Mom would be buried in Pennsylvania, there were dozens of details to plan: Where does the death certificate need to be sent? Do I send her clothes to the funeral director in Pennsylvania or in Tennessee? What about the pictures from which they will style her hair? (I liked the more natural look rather than the "gospel music bob" Mom sometimes wore.) How do I describe to the funeral director how I want my mom to look in the casket? Sometimes I'd feel guilty for even thinking such thoughts while Mom was so desperately clinging to life.

Dr. D'Amico visited Mom in her room, and checked her foot. She was cooperative, but when he bumped her good foot against the one that endured the amputations, she squawked, "Hey, there, buddy!"

The doctor apologized and we all laughed. She wasn't giving up yet.

Chapter 36

DOWN THE
HOMESTRETCH

D r. D'Amico had said that a refusal to eat commonly occurred with dementia patients heading down the homestretch. Because Mom had eaten a "full meal," I momentarily lulled myself into thinking that perhaps Mom wasn't really at that point yet, although I knew better.

Usually before leaving, I'd say, "I love you, Mom. See you later," and she responded similarly. But lately, she initiated the expression. "I'm going to go now," she said as she closed her eyes.

Each day, the pain intensified; I saw it in Mom's face and in her demeanor. The sores on her bottom broke open, leaving gaping holes in her skin, surrounded by blackened, bruised areas spreading out to pinkish-red areas. Even the slightest motion caused her to cringe.

Dressed only in a hospital gown and an adult diaper, she tried in vain to grasp my hand and reposition herself. At one point she looked up at me and said, "I miss my mom."

"I know, Mom," I replied. "So do I."

Since Mom was no longer able to eat in the dining room, the techs brought her dinner to her room. I cut some steamed carrots into quarter-inch pieces and tried to get Mom to eat them. Her lips refused to move. After I held the food to her lips for more than a minute or two, Mom said, "I need a bigger mouth."

Beginning in early July, Mom no longer got up, but remained in bed. Her entire body was hot. She rarely complained to us, but every few minutes she repeated, "Please Jesus, help me. Take away this pain, please Jesus."

"He will, Mom. He will," I said softly. *One day soon*, I thought, *He will indeed relieve you of the pain that is ravaging your body.*

"But I want Him to take away this pain now," she said, almost as if she could read my mind. For now I could do little but observe her suffering. It was a horrendously helpless feeling.

Again my mind defaulted to my questions. *Why must she endure this, Lord? For what purpose?* I knew that even if Mom rallied, her life would be more difficult than before. *What am I supposed to learn from all this, God? Maybe I'm to learn how a saint dies; perhaps I'm to learn how to be more compassionate with those who are hurting; maybe I'm to learn that this life is not all there is, that God has things in store for us that our eyes haven't seen or our minds yet conceived. Whatever it is that I'm supposed to learn, Lord, I wish you'd help me to learn it soon*, I prayed. I felt selfish instantly after my prayer, but it was an honest, sincere one.

By mid-July Mom was eating less than a few ounces a day, and the nurses had doubled her medications. Her legs were contracting into a rigid fetal position. She only reluctantly straightened them when she sat up in a wheelchair for an hour or so. She was very weak. One morning I stopped in to see her around 9:00, and the first thing she said to me as she grabbed my hand and squeezed tightly was, "I'm watching for Jesus. Where is He? When is He coming for me?"

Her statements caught me off guard. She looked at me almost impishly and whispered, "I have been a trooper, haven't I?"

I chuckled and said, "Yes, you have. And Jesus loves you."

Her parched lips formed a soft grin. "Yes, Jesus loves me. And I love Him." Then she added quietly, "Hallelujah."

Before I left I reminded Mom that Jesus could come for us at any time. She smiled weakly and said, "Oh, glory!" louder than the whisper with which she had been speaking. "What a day that will be! Hallelujah, I'm going to see kings and queens."

"Yes, you are, Mom."

"I'm ready to go, but I'm going to miss you and the other kids," she whispered and then paused, and I guessed that she was trying to remember all our family members. "Don't forget to thank the Lord for all the good times we've had together."

"I'll remember, Mom." It struck me that she had taught me how to live, and now she was teaching me how to die.

"I'm watching for Jesus," she said again. "I'm ready to roll."

"He'll be coming soon, Mom," I said as I quickly left the room so she wouldn't see me crying. It was hard to be sad when she was so ready to go.

Chapter 37

. . . .

THIS REALLY STINKS

Day after day Mom clung to life. In my mind I kept trying to let her go, but in my heart I wished that she could stay awhile longer.

One Saturday night she was in bed around seven o'clock, and Ruth, her roommate, was watching television when one of Bill Gaither's *Homecoming* programs came on the screen. Mom wasn't facing the television, but she could hear the music and she perked up. "That's good music," she said softly.

Near the end of the program the Gaither group performed "Sweet, Sweet Spirit," and the words to the song seemed especially poignant as she quietly mouthed each phrase to the ending chorus:

> *Without a doubt we'll know,*
> *That we have been revived,*
> *When we shall leave this place.[1]*

Mom was getting ready for the ultimate revival that, in many ways, had already begun in her life, but would be consummated the moment her spirit left Grace.

Before I left that night, Mom and I talked more about heaven, what it will look like and what we will do there.

"We'll have lots of time there. What do you want to do for the first thousand years?" I asked.

Without a moment's hesitation, Mom said, "We can sing glory be to the Lamb of God. Glory, glory to the Lamb. Hallelujah."

I nodded. "Yes, we can, Mom. Yes, we will."

Earlier that day she had displayed a glint of her sense of humor when she told Nurse Pam, "I want to see Jesus."

"You can go to Jesus, Minnie," Pam said. "It's okay."

"I want to," Mom replied, "but my body won't let me."

I met informally with Nurse Pam, and we decided it was time to move to a slow-release morphine patch, which would provide more consistent pain relief than other forms of pain meds given every six hours. I knew the medication would knock Mom out, where she could barely communicate, but I felt that it was selfish of me to want otherwise.

We also concluded that it was unnecessary for the techs to get Mom up, dressed, and seated in the wheelchair. Being lifted in and out of bed was one of the few things Mom complained about these days. "Please don't do that," she'd beg. "Please don't move me around like that."

"We're sorry, but we have to get you up, Miss Minnie," the nurses apologized. "You'll feel better once we get you situated." It was awful to observe.

"Unless she is having a good day, and wants to sit up," I told Pam, "I'm okay with her staying in bed. She doesn't need to get up simply for my benefit, to visit with me."

I wasn't quite sure how to phrase it without sounding calloused and insensitive, but from a logistical standpoint, I wanted to know what kind of time Pam thought we might have. "From your experience, and seeing this sort of situation, can you draw any conclusions about how much time we have left with my mom?"

"It's hard to tell, but the way her skin is blotching, she will probably die from the sores before the bone infection does its worst. Those kinds of wounds can turn septic almost overnight, and if that happens, we're probably looking at less than a week."

I nodded, the reality of Pam's words searing into my heart and mind. "Are there any telltale signs of which we should be aware?" I asked.

"If her temperature spikes, that is certainly an indicator. Right now her vital signs and pulse and blood pressure are good. So we'll just have to keep a close watch on her."

I thanked Pam for her help in caring for my mom, and especially the spiritual values she brought to her work. "As you know, not all hospices are so overt about spiritual matters. They will talk about having a higher power, but they don't point people to Jesus. My mom's faith is not in a religion; it is in Jesus Christ. To separate her dying from her faith in Christ would be foolish."

"I agree, Ken, and we will be sensitive to that. Your mom is a strong believer, and I haven't sensed a bit of fear in her. Every day she talks about Jesus. She has little strength left, but she's using what she has to talk about Jesus. I guess that shouldn't surprise any of us."

When I went back in to check on her, Mom's body was extremely warm.

"Do you hurt any place?" I asked.

"I hurt all over," she said quietly.

I believed her. I placed my hand on her forehead and prayed, "Lord Jesus, please help Mom to feel better. Please heal her and take away this headache." I wasn't praying that God would cause my mom to get up and walk out of the nursing home. I was just asking that He would ease her pain.

As she often did, Mom confused me with my dad. "Oh, Daddy," she said as she squeezed my hand. "If I could just be rid of this headache."

I prayed for Mom again, and lowered the angle on her hospital bed so she could rest her head on the pillow. Night was closing in, and our time together was rapidly coming to an end.

There is an emotional toll to this long, drawn-out ordeal that I'm reluctant to admit, much less mention, but it is quite real. In a nutshell, the visits with my mom at this stage were as emotionally painful for me as they were physically painful for her. Seeing her grimace in pain, and not being able to do anything about it, other than to ask the nurse for more medication, was a terribly helpless place to be. Trying to feed her, coaxing each drop of water and each minuscule morsel of food into her mouth, often for more than an hour at a time, was an exercise in futility and fatigue. I left Grace each day totally drained, feeling as though someone unscrewed my feet and emptied me of every bit of energy.

When friends asked me how my mom was doing, they frequently followed with, "And how are you doing?" Usually I tried to be positive.

"Mom seems ready to go to heaven," I'd say, "and that's the best that I could hope for her." But in my most honest moments, I'd admit to myself, *This really stinks.*

It wasn't fair to Mom for me to complain or soak in self-pity.

She was the one in real pain, whose body was racked with infection and fever, whose little toes were turning to black ashes, emitting a grotesque smell—the smell of death, one orderly commented; she was the one dying. But I'd be less than honest if I didn't admit that often when sitting with her, watching her barely able to gasp for breath or twitching involuntarily, hardly conscious, I'd pray, *God, as much as I will miss her when she's gone, this is no life for her. What does all this mean? Why must she suffer this pain and indignity? For whose benefit? Mine? The people here at the nursing home? Certainly not for Mom's benefit. It just doesn't make sense.*

Whether the inner voice came from the Spirit of God, or simply my own ruminations, I heard a reassuring voice: "All my life, Mom taught me how to live. Now she is teaching me how to die."

When her tech and I tried to move Mom on the bed, so she could sit up to attempt to eat something, Mom shrieked in pain. "No!"

"I'm sorry, Mom," I replied. "We're just trying to help you."

"No, please!" she cried out again. We finally got her situated on her back, and she said quietly, "I just can't stand it any more." It was heart-wrenching.

Mom's lips were parched, just as the hospice nurses warned they might be during the final days of her life. The nurses brought in small foam swabs so I could dip a swab in some water and run it over Mom's lips, hopefully dripping the water onto her tongue and to her throat. It was a tedious process, and I got more water on Mom than in her mouth. I felt terrible for inflicting any further pain on her than she was already experiencing, but I could tell she hadn't been drinking any water so we had to get her up. It was risky enough trying to feed her as she reclined in bed, since her ability to swallow was negligible. Any of the soft, mushy food I was able to get into her mouth could easily stick in her throat and choke her to death. How awful would that be, if after surviving all that she had, that her son would cause her death by feeding her too large a glob of cottage cheese.

Mom was scratching her hip and there were several open sores in that area so I gently moved her hand to another location on her upper thigh. When I did, I was shocked to discover that her entire thigh had atrophied, shriveled up, and almost disappeared! I could encompass her leg using my two hands, and if I wrapped my hands around her thigh, my fingertips could touch without squeezing her skin. Her upper thigh felt as thin as her forearm once was; she looked like a person you might see in a country ravaged by famine, her body dwindled to nothing but skin and bones. Again I prayed, *How long, Lord? How long?*

Chapter 38

LAST CALL

When the telephone rang at 5:25 in the morning on July 27, I instinctively knew Mom's ordeal was over. It was the inevitable call I didn't want to receive.

A nurse from Grace was on the line. "Ken, I think this may be the day for Miss Minnie. She's had a difficult night."

"I understand," I said. "Should I come right now?"

"Yes, please."

Just then Pam came on the phone. "Ken, she's not breathing," she said. "She's gone."

"I'll be right there, Pam." Lisa and I threw on our clothes and raced across town. Thanks to the early hour, traffic was still light, so we arrived at Grace within minutes. Pam met us in the hallway and hugged us tightly.

We entered Mom's room as quietly as possible to avoid waking Ruth, Mom's roommate. Ruth had left her television on a music network overnight, so somebody was crooning a country song when my eyes first saw my deceased mother.

She was dressed only in a nightgown. Her face was slightly contorted, and her legs were drawn up under her as they had been for nearly two months now. Other than that, she looked peaceful. I leaned over her bed and hugged her. She was still warm. "I love you, Mom."

I had done the same thing the night before, putting my face next to hers. Usually when I did that, she'd kiss me and whisper hoarsely, "I love you, son." The last night before I left, she mouthed the words, but no sound came out. Earlier that evening, I'd tried to get her to eat some ice cream. But it simply stayed on her tongue and clogged her lips until it melted; she couldn't swallow. I'd quickly taken a tissue and wiped the ice cream out of her mouth.

When I'd left that night, I had leaned over to kiss mom good-bye, and as I always did, I'd said, "I'll see you tomorrow." In my mind, I added the words, *One way or the other,* dead or alive. I knew we were near the end, but Mom had surprised us so many times before, I didn't feel compelled to sit with her throughout the night.

I'd waved good-bye one last time before slipping quietly out of her room.

Now it was morning, and Mom was gone. Lisa and I waited quietly with Mom's still body, sure that her spirit was already in heaven. Slowly, almost imperceptibly, her skin turned cooler, then ice-cold. Sitting there, waiting for the coroner and the mortician to arrive, I stared at Mom's form on the bed. Did I really believe what we proclaimed, that she was still alive, that we would see her again in heaven? I had always loved the story of evangelist D.L. Moody, who wrote while he was still living, "Some day you will read in the papers that D.L. Moody, of East Northfield, is dead. Don't you believe a word of it! At that moment, I shall be more alive than I am now, I shall have gone up higher, that is all. . . ."[1]

I knew my mom believed in heaven; she'd taught her family to do the same, and except for a few bouts of vacillating faith during my collegiate years, I rarely allowed doubts about the Bible to turn into unbelief. Now as I stared at Mom's dead body, I asked myself again, *Is it real? Is there really a heaven? Or is this it? Her life is over, and except for a few days of remembrance at her funeral, and her good influence in the lives of others, this is all she wrote. Is it true that, as the apostle Paul believed—to be absent from the body was to be present with the Lord? Or is that nothing more than Christian schmaltz?*

But as I gazed at my mom's motionless form, I knew she believed—how could I not believe? My questions and doubts soon gave way to a trust and peace. Yes, I believed. I believed more now than ever.

As much as we had prepared for this day, it was still emotionally overwhelming. When the mortician asked if we needed more time with my mom, I cringed. "No, we're ready," I said.

That was a lie. How could anyone ever be ready for a moment like this? I looked in another direction as the nurses and mortician picked up my mom's body from the bed and slid her onto a gurney. They covered her completely with a sheet before taking her out of the room.

I watched, trembling, as the mortician wheeled my mom down the hallway toward the hearse. I continued watching—much like she had watched me leaving so many times—until they made the turn and were out of sight. Tears flowed freely as some of the Grace nurses, technicians, and staff hugged me, telling me what a wonderful influence my mom had been. It was difficult to be sad in the face of such marvelous compliments and testimonies.

I called my brothers with the news. "This is the call you didn't want to get," I began. "But she's not in any more pain. In fact, she's doing better than ever."

"Never better," Mom would say.

Chapter 39

THE HAUNTING,
UNSPOKEN QUESTIONS

People traveled from miles around and from several states away to attend Mom's "homegoing" celebration. During the service John gave testimony of how he found the Lord, thanks to Mom. Tink and I shared some of our special memories. Other guests spontaneously stood to bear witness of Mom's influence in their lives. One fellow told how nearly thirty years earlier, when performing in a country band with his life falling apart, he saw Mom onstage. He committed his life to Christ that night and had been serving God through his music and business ever since. He had driven four hours that day to honor the woman who influenced him to follow Jesus. The funeral was a marvelous tribute to a little woman whose only distinctions were her love for the Lord and her love for people.

For the next few days, it seemed as though my car wanted to

automatically drive to Grace. I saw reminders of my mom everywhere. At odd times, messages from Mom that I had saved on my voice mail over the past four years popped up on my cell phone.

"Ken, I'm here at Graceland," Mom's voice reminded me. "I'm here, you know, at that place where I work," she added. Some of the messages struck me as almost spooky, others evoked strong emotional responses, some were funny, some comforting.

One of Mom's recorded messages caught me emotionally off-guard when I heard it. My outgoing cell phone message encourages callers to leave a call-back number, so in a laconic tone of voice, Mom responded to my message: "Ken, I don't have a call-back number."

Little things touched emotional chords in me. Driving to church, for example, I noticed the clock in the car, and realized that was the time we had picked up my mom to take her with us to church. I bounced back and forth across a wide spectrum of thoughts and emotions. I flip-flopped from a peaceful resignation to a reccurring need to talk about my mom, to a deep sadness and restlessness, to waking up in the middle of the night seeing her in pain, to a complete confidence knowing she was with the Lord and totally healed. I tossed and turned all night, and then experienced a listless lack of energy all day long. Because Mom's death was not unexpected—we had, after all, been moving inexorably toward the end of her life on earth for several years—these responses to grief surprised me. In talking with others who had lost a parent, I discovered that my reactions were not unusual. Professional counselors suggest that healing from grief often takes more than a year. I knew it would take time, but hoped that I could lessen that learning curve.

My most recurring thought was: *How am I supposed to feel now that Mom is gone?* Of course I knew there was no pat answer, but that didn't dispel the wondering.

Everywhere I went, folks offered kind words of encouragement, a pertinent verse of Scripture, or a sweet sentiment about my mom.

Trying to answer all the cards, letters, and e-mails we received was almost a full-time job, but I wanted well-wishers to know their expressions meant much to my family. People who knew the vigil we had been keeping often fumbled for words in expressing their condolences. I understood. I'd been on that side of the equation many times. One friend posed an unsettling thought: "You have been running constantly taking care of Minnie," he said, "visiting with her every day at the nursing home. You must feel relieved now."

Relieved?

That word had never crossed my mind. If the person meant that I was relieved Mom was no longer suffering, relieved that she was now in heaven with the Lord she loved, yes, I was relieved. If he meant that I was now unencumbered by a heavy load, his statement would imply a misconception. I wasn't forced to take care of my mom as she journeyed through dementia; I was glad to do so. I did the best I could to honor my mother, fulfilling my responsibilities as a son until the moment the cemetery workers lowered her into the ground and covered the casket with freshly dug dirt.

Relieved? I guess so; now that I was no longer traipsing back and forth to the nursing home, I had a few extra hours every day to work. But I have the rest of my life to work—I had Mom with us for only a few precious years. Admittedly, it is never easy to care for an aging parent, especially when your parent has become your child. But it is not a relief when he or she is gone. It is a calm satisfaction in knowing that you did your best. It is a privilege to have served!

So what did we learn from Mom's experience, and what tips worked best for us? Mostly we discovered that we were not dealing with stubbornness, rudeness, or insubordination on the part of an aging parent—we were confronting a powerful disease that was incrementally taking control of our mom's brain. I've sprinkled indicators of Alzheimer's and dementia throughout these pages, and if you notice these characteristics in your loved one, it would be worth a check-up. Here are a few that we encountered:

- Memory problems, inability to remember names, people, or events in recent history
- Combativeness in conversations
- Loss of coordination, especially eye-hand coordination; slowing reflexes, bumps and falls
- Confusion over days and time
- Unwarranted fears and suspicions
- Overreactions, emotional outbursts, uncharacteristic profanity, and loss of "filters"
- Hoarding, stealing, and possessiveness
- Urinary incontinence
- Unusual moodiness, boredom, or inability to follow a story
- Loss of appetite

Scientists also believe that one of the first areas of the brain affected by Alzheimer's is the sense of smell. If your loved one has difficulty recognizing the aromas from roses, peppermint, leather, pineapple, natural gas, smoke, or lemons, it may indicate a disruption in the brain's hippocampus, the area where such memories are stored.

The most helpful tips I can pass along to anyone caring for a parent who has become a child include:

- Don't argue, but change the subject. This really worked!
- Don't try to shame or lecture your parent into doing what is best for them; distract, divert attention, and do what has to be done.

- Avoid the word *remember*. Instead reminisce with your loved one, remind and reassure.
- Physical touch is important.
- Monitor medications!
- Get rid of clutter. Simplify even family photos.
- Make spiritual input a priority. Worship together, read Scripture, sing. Even if you can't carry a tune, the words of those songs can still lift a heart.
- Take care of yourself. You can only do so much. There is no shame in asking for help.
- Pray—for strength and patience, but also prayers of thankfulness for giving you the opportunity to bless your parent.
- Celebrate everything you can!

What about me? Am I susceptible to Alzheimer's and dementia since my mother suffered from them? Probably so. Age and genetics are stacked against me. But my faith helps me to hope for the best, and I am determined to do my part by maintaining a healthy lifestyle.

A few months before Mom passed away, Dr. D'Amico attended a conference on the hereditary aspects of Alzheimer's. I had high hopes that he'd return with conclusive evidence of a genetic relationship between parents who have dementia, the potential of their children developing dementia, and a plan to prevent it. He didn't. Instead, the information pool becomes increasingly muddy with each new study. "Alzheimer's can be delayed with squirt of insulin," one recent study reported.[1] "High cholesterol tied to Alzheimer's," another study concluded.[2] Yet another study revealed that a cancer drug, bexarotene, temporarily reversed the effects of Alzheimer's—in mice.[3]

Information about Alzheimer's is freely available online, but much of it is contradictory, so beware the latest headlines touting breakthroughs and cures. The truth is, medical science still does not know what causes Alzheimer's and dementia, or how to cure them. A sticky protein, beta-amyloid, is currently considered the culprit most often linked with Alzheimer's. Beta-amyloid is produced naturally by your body, but too much of it can produce a goo in your brain that clogs synapses and thwarts communication between neurons, causing forgetfulness. Research is ongoing, and scientists are hopeful, but right now we're still in the dark.

So what can you do to stave off Alzheimer's and dementia? Basically the same things you should do to prevent obesity, heart disease, diabetes, and other debilitating diseases. Exercise helps, but eating right is the key. A diet rich in antioxidants, including plenty of colorful fruits, and omega-3 fats, which can be found in nuts, avocados, and grilled fish such as halibut, salmon, and anchovies (sorry, no fried fish), can strengthen brain cells and help you avoid Alzheimer's. Baked potatoes are good; French fries are a no-no. Curry and spices, even a few cups of coffee per day may reduce your risk of Alzheimer's. Cholesterol-lowering foods such as pistachio nuts, whole oranges (rather than orange juice), oatmeal, beans, and garlic are also helpful in controlling your body's production of beta-amyloid, which may lower your chances of Alzheimer's.

Keeping up levels of acetylcholine (a neurotransmitter) by eating plenty of organic whole eggs, yogurt, turkey, chicken, and leafy greens slows cognitive decline. Supplements such as lecithin are thought to lower cholesterol, which helps in fighting Alzheimer's.

The Alzheimer's Association suggests maintaining four simple habits:

1. Stay physically active. Physical exercise helps to maintain good blood flow to the brain and encourages the growth of new brain cells.

2. Eat a healthy diet. High cholesterol may contribute to strokes and brain cell damage, so follow a low-fat, low-cholesterol diet.
3. Remain socially active. Social activity can reduce stress levels, which helps maintain healthy connections among brain cells.
4. Stay mentally active. Read, write, work puzzles. Word games such as Scrabble or number challenges like Sudoku are helpful. Mentally stimulating activities strengthen brain cells and the connections between them and may even create new nerve cells.[4]

The Alzheimer's Association's advice to eat right, ingest lots of antioxidants, stay healthy, avoid overweight issues, get plenty of exercise—all the usual stuff—offers great hope that we can avoid dementia. Knowing the risk factors, we'd be foolish to ignore the preventative measures. The worst thing we can do is nothing.

Can I prepare? Yes. Frank discussions among family members and contingency planning can help. Emotional and spiritual preparation is essential, and we dare not ignore the financial aspects either. It is an accepted fact that most of our medical expenses will be incurred during the final few years of life. Financial counselor Dave Ramsey recommends nursing home insurance for anyone over sixty years of age because the costs of long-term care in an assisted-living or skilled-care facility can break you or decimate a family member's nest egg. Granted, such insurance could be a waste of money for many people, but if you need it, it will be worth every penny.

Lately I've been working with Mom's glasses resting on my desk, just below my computer screen. I placed her glasses there intentionally, along with a wooden "bone" that she gave to our lovable toy poodle, Pumpkin, for Christmas one year. The full name of

Pumpkin wouldn't fit on the bone, so Mom had simply abbreviated the name to "Pumkin." Although Mom had no knowledge of it, that's how our daughter Megan had always spelled Pumpkin's name. Pumpkin was a special part of our family. I referred to him as my "writing assistant," since he'd often sit at my feet under my desk—when he couldn't beg his way into my lap—while I wrote.

Occasionally I had taken him with me when I had visited Mom at Grace. She loved holding Pumpkin in her lap, cuddling her little buddy as she sat in her wheelchair. When Pumpkin passed away, I didn't have the heart to tell Mom. She loved that dog and they had entered into the dementia years together. So I've kept Mom's glasses and Pumpkin's bone on my desk as two reminders of their unconditional love, almost as though they are still with me, helping me write—which, I suppose, in a way, they are.

In moments of reflection since Mom's passing, I've wondered what she was trying to teach us during those final years. What wisdom did she want to impart to us, and to others, before she left this world? What really mattered to her as she headed toward home? I think I know, and I guess that's why I've felt compelled to share this story. By traveling with Mom through the netherworld of dementia, I found the realities of faith—Mom's and my own—to be tested and true.

Our journey through dementia is not unique, nor is it the most dramatic. I've heard horror stories from friends who have walked with their parents into the same sort of role reversal, and they have nightmares just thinking about some of the twists and turns their parents took in their final stages of Alzheimer's. Our story is not a perfect package, but then life with an aging parent is never about developing perfect solutions. It is about doing the best you can to love your family member and to care for him or her with what limited time and resources you have.

Of this I am sure: One of these days, we are going to be reunited with our loved ones who trusted in Jesus, and we will receive His promised reward. I can imagine that first day in heaven, after I've seen Jesus, when I find my mom in the crowd of worshippers. I can hear me saying to her, "Mom, thank you! You helped me to get here! Because of your prayers, your sacrificial commitment, your love, I entrusted my life to Jesus Christ. And now we're here together!"

I can see us hugging on streets of gold, and hear myself saying, "I love you, Mom. Tell me; is heaven all that you thought it would be? How are you doing? How are you feeling?"

With her toes and feet restored and all signs of dementia and Alzheimer's banished forever, I can imagine Mom raising her hands in praise and adoration of Jesus, opening her arms as though inviting me to view the sweeping, mind-boggling panorama all around us.

You know what her answer will be.

"Never better!"

Notes

Chapter 22

1. Elizabeth Cohen, "How to Limit Alzheimer's Wandering," CNN Health, posted Thursday, November 10, 2011, http://www.cnn.com/2011/11/10/health/alzheimers-lost-empowered-patient/index.html.

Chapter 37

1. Doris Akers, "Sweet, Sweet Spirit," 1962.

Chapter 38

1. William R. Moody, *The Autobiography of Dwight L. Moody* (New York: Fleming H. Revell Company, 1900), preface, 1.

Chapter 39

1. Gina Kolata, "A Squirt of Insulin May Delay Alzheimer's," *New York Times*, September 12, 2011, http://nytimes.com/2011/09/13/health/research/13alzheimers.html?_r=1&pagewante . . . 9/14/2011.
2. "High Cholesterol Tied to Alzheimer's," Newsmax Health, posted Tuesday, September 13, 2011, http://www.newsmaxhealth.com/health_stories/Cholesterol_Alzheimers/2011/09/13/406916.html.

3. David Brown, "Cancer Drug Shows Promise in Mouse Alzheimer's Study," *The Washington Post*, February 9, 2012, http://www .washingtonpost.com/national/health-science/cancer -drug-shows-promise-in-mouse-alzheimers-study/2012/02/09 /gIQAzJct1Q_story.html.

4. Alzheimer's Association, "Brain Health," accessed March 22, 2012, http://www.alz.org/we_can_help_brain_health_maintain_your _brain.asp.

ABOUT THE AUTHOR

Ken Abraham is a *New York Times* best-selling author known around the world for his collaborations with high-profile public figures. A former professional musician and pastor, he is a popular guest with both secular and religious media. His books include *One Soldier's Story* with Bob Dole, *Payne Stewart* with Tracey Stewart, *Falling in Love for All the Right Reasons* with Dr. Neil Clark Warren, and *Let's Roll!* with Lisa Beamer.